Final Warning of Climate Change:

Dreams, Visions, and Revelations.

By John A. Hodge

FOREWORD

This book, Final Warning of Climate Change; Dreams, Visions, and Revelations, is written for all men. God has seen our attitude of unthankfulness, our waywardness, and the hardening of our hearts to Him. He sees us ignoring His warnings, serving and worshipping strange gods and idols, and being deceived by Satan. We are privileged to be able to receive constant warnings from God. His Word is preached in so many ways, reminding us of God's free gift of salvation and helping us to escape the awful wrath of God's punishment. One of his warnings is in the form of "climate change."

Jesus' coming is very near and this could happen at any moment; therefore, I am encouraging all men everywhere to consider your ways and be wise. Stop whatever you are doing, look at the dangers ahead, listen to the messengers of God, give attention to His written word, and, finally, give Him your hearts.

ABOUT THE AUTHOR

T his book is written by John Adolphus Hodge. I am a Christian, and I gave my heart to the Lord at the age of thirteen. I am from a family of eight, consisting of four boys and four girls, of which I am the third born and the first son. I am blessed with two loving children, Lynelle (daughter) and Tristan (son), and one happy grandson, Landon, who delights in praising the Lord.

I worked in the field of construction, but specialised in carpentry, both rough and fine work. I spent a lot of time in joinery, which entails furniture building. I love my work and it was my delight to see the finished product—a beautiful piece of furniture.

In the year 2005, the Lord did a U-turn and destroyed my life compass, replacing it with His own. This dramatic change confused families and friends. I, however, was never deterred because on every step of the journey, I experienced the hand and work of God in full control. This new direction consisted of on the job training, migrating to other islands and countries, and visiting special churches. These actions prepared me to have a better knowledge of the Word of God, enabling me to fulfil His will, plans, and purpose for which I was born.

John Adolphus Hodge

INTRODUCTION

It was "Decision Time." At this stage of my life, I was all alone, and I came face to face with Mr. Loneliness. Loneliness is one of man's greatest tests as he journeys throughout the different stages of life. In the short term, it is brain-searching, heart-warming, nerve-relaxing, and a good medication for all men at intervals of life. It is the experienced of having a cold shower after a hot, hard, long day at work.

On the other hand, long-term loneliness is a form of physical, social, and mental imprisonment. It depicts a person's sentence for a crime committed, having shackles roughly placed on his hands, and having the 'Iron Gate' close mercilessly with the keys thrown away. At this critical time of life, I had to make my choice. I had to choose between the positive road of life and the negative road of life.

Finally, I prayed to God for His help, direction, and guidance as I chose the positive road of life, which consists of constant prayer and fasting. This opens my spiritual ears, eyes, heart, and mind to the voice of God the Holy Spirit as He clearly speaks to me. Giving Him time and space to guide me into the right direction, in line with His will, plans, and purposes for my life. His plans were drawn up long before the world began.

This book, Final Warning of Climate Change: Dreams, Visions, and Revelations, is about how God the Holy Spirit is in full control, demonstrating to mankind His Unconditional Love for us in spite of our stubborn attitude, unthankfulness, and refusal to give Him our undivided attention. God is merciful and He is here, demonstrating to us the fullness of His Love. God's love passes or supersedes the knowledge of mankind. This is why His Love is described as ever-lasting, boundless, and never-ending. Only God can perfectly demonstrate such love.

Although mankind still refuses to give God his listening ears, He still loves us and always sends us warnings long before judgment and destructions. Before destruction and judgment on the city of Nineveh, God send His messenger, but the people (like the majority today) refused to listen to the message he brought to them and they perished. Everyone knows about Noah, whom God send with the Final Message to the people in his days. They refused to listen to both the message and the messenger, from God in His Love to mankind. These people perished in the flood because they were too ignorant and arrogant to give God their listening ears and they perished.

In the days of Noah, God sent His "Final Messenger, with the Final Warning," but the people were caught up in the excitements of life and its surroundings. The topic of Noah's of message was "climate change," God allowed him to preached for one hundred and twenty years on this one topic, but the people ignorantly refused to listen, not knowing their fate. These people were privileged, and like us, they had a faithful servant of God, begging them to listen to their last message, because he was indeed the last messenger, preaching the last topic of the danger and destruction of climate change. These busy, party, business, smart folks, were walking the last mile of their life, enjoying their last time of fun and finally were perished in the flood of climate change. Oh, how foolish!

Today, we are a most privilege people, because we had those people in Noah's days as our example. Are we going to be ignorant, arrogant, and foolish like those people, refusing to listen to the same message, our final message, and the message of judgment and destruction of climate change? Jesus is coming very soon, this could be at any moment, all God the Father is asking us to do is simply accept His Son Jesus as our Saviour and be saved from the death and destruction climate change is bringing upon you. Avoid listening to Satan, who is saying, "Leave that for later. You still have lots time remaining." Are you going to wait, like those people, until you see the rain and begin to fall? Are you going to wait until the seas turn jet black to believe? Then it will be too late, because God's door of mercy for you will then be closed! Are you waiting to see the appearance of Jesus in the sky (the rapture), collecting His dear Saints? It will be too late! Give your heart to Jesus now and all will be well. You will enjoy eternal life with God the Father, God the Son, God the Holy Spirit, the Angels, and all Children of God. You will avoid the awful wrath of hell!

This Book is dedicated to our dear Loving Mother and Father.

My loving mother, at a tender age, laid a solid foundation for me, built on Jesus Christ our Lord. She expressed her love for the Lord by taking her children to Church and Sunday school. There, I heard the Word of God and gave my heart to the Lord at the age of thirteen. I vividly remember when I surrendered my heart to the Lord one Sunday night in May, 1967, after hearing the Gospel preached by the evangelist T.C. Taylor.

After many years of serving the Lord, I attended a crusade and received a Word of Prophecy from God the Holy Spirit through the Evangelist Reverend Rita Partin Spaulding of Tennessee, USA. At that time, God made a dramatic turn in my life, destroying all of my plans and replacing them with His plans. I pray that as you read these urgent warnings of God the Holy Spirit, you will consider the condition of your soul and give your heart to God by accepting His Son, Jesus, as your Saviour.

FINAL WARNING OF CLIMATE CHANGE: DREAMS, VISIONS, AND REVELATIONS.

J ohn 10:9 reads, "That if thou shalt confess with thy mouth the Lord Jesus, and shalt believe in thine heart that God hath raised him from the dead, thou shalt be saved."

This is the confession of my parents. I remembered their words of faith and their trust in God through the redemptive power of the blood of Jesus, which He shed on the cross, once and for all for the whole world, cleansing us while we believed. John 14:1–9, also reads,

> Let not your heart be troubled: ye believe in God, believe also in me. In my Father's house are many mansions: if it were not so, I would have told you. I go to prepare a place for you. And if I go and prepare a place for you, I will come again, and receive you unto myself; that where I am, there ye may be also. And whither I go ye know, and the way ye know. Thomas saith unto him, Lord, we know not whither thou goest; and how can we know the way? Jesus saith unto him, I am the way, the truth, and the life: no man cometh unto the Father, but by me. If ye had known me, ye should have known my Father also: and from hence-forth ye know him, and have seen him.

> Philip saith unto him, Lord, show us the Father, and
> it sufficeth us. Jesus saith unto him, have I been so
> long time with you, and yet hast thou not known me,
> Philip? he that hath seen me hath seen the Father; and
> how sayest thou then, Show us the Father?

My parents were born on the beautiful island of St. Kitts, Leeward Islands. They were born of Kittitian and Anguillan parentage and were married and blessed with eight wonderful children; four girls and four boys.

Our loving mother was not a born again child of God when we were born, but, interestingly, most of her children were blessed with biblical names: Jean, Melvina, John, Joseph, Stanley, Moses, Brenda, and Esther.

At the age of nine or ten, I saw a change in our mother when she started taking us to church and Sunday-school. She also developed a schedule for Bible devotions, which continued even after leaving school. We were sometimes laughed at by our school friends, because while they played games we had to head home for devotions. During our sessions of devotions, we were taught to memorize Bible verses and were trained to lead devotions.

Our mother, taught us to give God thanks when we woke up and before we went to bed. It was our duty to thank God for His goodness, mercy and protection throughout the day.

Her devotion to God extended outside the home to the public streets, the hospitals, the old aged homes and private homes where she shared the message of God. My mother would also spread the gospel to friends and surrounding neighbours. This resulted in countless people giving their hearts and lives to God. My mother undertook these duties faithfully until she departed this life.

My mother knew her time was drawing near, a few weeks before saying goodbye; she admonished each one of us to memorize Bible verses. Proverbs 22:6 "Train up a child in the way he should go: and when he is old, he will not depart from it."

Deuteronomy 4:9 "Only take heed to thyself, and keep thy soul diligently, lest thou forget the things which thine eyes have seen, and lest they depart from thy heart all the days of thy life: but teach them to thy son, and thy sons' sons'; Specially the day that thou stoodest before the Lord thy God in Horeb, when the Lord said unto me, Gather me the people together, and I will make them hear my words, that they may learn to fear me all the days that they shall live upon the earth, and that they may teach their children."

I memorized these scriptures and I am now receiving great rewards of divine blessings from God in the form of dreams, visions and revelations, some of which He commanded me to share with you in this book.

Mommy passed away on February 8th, 2004, and said goodbye to this world while quietly singing her way into the presence of God. It was an unforgettable day. Our loving mother is not dead; she is just silently sleeping. We are all awaiting that grand family reunion when Jesus comes in the Rapture, for all His remaining children. Before our loving mother died, she had the privilege of seeing her children give their lives to Jesus! It is now our turn to continue her legacy, witnessing to our families and ensuring they too trust Jesus as their Saviour.

Our father, Wilfred Adolphus Hodge, died in Birmingham, UK, in April, 2012 where he lived and worked for fifty-three years. He was a wonderful father with an unblemished record of a great provider. When he resided in the UK, he would occasionally visit us and always kept in touch.

Our daddy was a very quiet, kind-hearted, and soft-spoken person with a passion for music. He played both the keyboard and the trumpet for many years, bringing joy and gladness to many hearts. He was also blessed with a rich tenor voice, which he made good use of at weddings, churches, special gatherings, and even on the phone for birthdays. Daddy had something truly special about him that the opposite sex could never resist. His was a handsome gentleman, well dressed, and had a distinction in doing so. He also loved to cook and did a good job at it.

We loved both our parents dearly thank you Mommy and Daddy, we all Love you; our love for you will never die! God's forever blessings!

ACKNOWLEDGMENT

Thanks to:
God The Father
God The Son
God The Holy Spirit.

Thanks to my Loving Mother, Mrs. Dolly Agatha Henrietta Hodge, who was our mentor, a God bless mother, An Angel of Love Sent from Heaven above. "So teach us to number our days, that we may apply our hearts unto wisdom." (Ps. 90:12).

To our Wonderful Daddy-Fred, Mr. Wilfred Adolphus Hodge, who was a faithful father with an unblemished record of a great provider. "Cast not away therefore your confidence, which hath great recompense of reward" (Heb. 10:35).

To Lynelle and Merle Hodge who assist me with most of the editing, to you I say, "Thanks and God's forever blessings!" "If ye shall ask any thing in my name, I will do it" (John 14:14).

To Pastor Bishop Evangelists, and Rev Rita Partin Spaulding, of Tennessee, USA. Who is an International Crusade speaker, Founder of the Voice of Deliverance Bible College and The Cupbearer Ministry. Who in October, 2005, obediently hearing from God The Holy Spirit, and prophetically prophecy over my life. To you and family I say thanks! "And the people said unto Joshua, The LORD our God will we serve, and his voice will we obey" (Josh. 24:24).

To Pastor Gaston 'Ned' Harris and family, who lovingly fix my computer, free of cost (F.O.C). This I know is the favour of God and to him I say, "God keep His promises forever." To you and family I say, "And Jabez called on the God of Israel, saying, Oh that thou wouldest bless me indeed, and enlarged my coast, and that thine hand might be with me, and that thou wouldest keep me from evil, that it may not grieve me! And God granted him that which he requested" (1 Chron. 4:10). Thank you!

To Mr. Patrick James, Challengers Village, St. Kitts. West Indies. Thanks for teaching me the skills, fundamentals, and technology of computer. 'Except the LORD build the house, they labour in vain that build it: "Except the LORD keep the city, the watchman waketh but in vain" (Ps. 127:1).

To the late Pastor Dr. Ambrose Richardson, family and members of The Christian Fellowship Church, Anguilla, West Indies. Thanks for your messages of courage, personal help and hospitality. "This is the LORD'S doing: it is marvellous in our eyes" (Ps. 118:23).

> To all the Pastors, chosen by God The Holy Spirit, pre-paring, aiding and helping me with spiritual food for new directions consisted of on the job training, during migrating to other islands and countries and visiting special churches. These actions prepared me, to have a better knowledge of the Word of God, enabling me to fulfil destiny of His; will, plans and purpose for which I was born. Pastors: Pastor Bishop Evangelists and Rev Rita Partin Spaulding of Tennessee, USA. Pastor Bishop Gladstone Hazel, The Christian Fellowship Church, St. Thomas, U.S.V.I. Pastor Lincoln Hazell, Apostolic Faith Church, Basseterre, St. Kitts. Pastor the late Stanley Edwards, Apostolic Church, Sandy Point, St. Kitts. Pastor Paul Andrews, Apostolic Faith, Antigua. Pastor Dr. Ambrose Richardson, The Christian Fellowship Church, Anguilla. Pastor Cassius Feare, Pastor Mitchell and Pastor Pringle, of The Victory Tabernacle Church of IProphecy, Grand Cayman. Pastor Reverend Christian Weaver, Pilgrim Church, Nottingham, and U K. "In hope of eternal

life, which God, that cannot lie, promise before the world began" (Titus 1:2).

To Mrs. Omaha Richardson, Mrs. Wilma Harris and Mrs. Monique Richardson, Anguilla. Mrs. Angela Richardson, St. Kitts. Mrs. Dean Horsford, St. Thomas, USVI. Ms. Sylvia Burleigh, Xulon Press Christian Publishing, Florida, USA. Thanks for all roles played in the success of this book. 'She openeth her mouth with wisdom; and in her tongue is the law of kindness" (Prov. 31:26).

To all family, friends and well-wishers, I say many thanks! "If ye abide in me, and my words abide in in you, ye shall ask what ye will, and it shall be done unto you" (John 15:7).

GIVE THANKS = MEANS.

God The Father, God The Son, God The Holy Spirit:
Incarnate, Victorious, Eternal, Truly Holy Almighty, Nazarene
King, Sovereign-Saviour.

G = God The Father, God The Son, God The Holy Spirit.
I = Incarnate Trinity forever and ever,
V = Victorious Incarnate forever and ever,
E = Eternal Victorious forever and ever,

T = Truly Eternal forever and ever,
H = Holy Truly forever and ever,
A = Almighty Holy forever and ever,
N = Nazarene Almighty forever and ever,
K = King Nazarene forever and ever,
S = Sovereign King forever and ever, Amen.

People, let us give thanks! Give Thanks!
Give Thanks to God The Father, God The Son, God The Holy Spirit!
The Trinity is forever WORTHY!

To My Wonderful Dad.

Thank you for being a Father,
Who fears the Lord.
Your example has taught me,

So many Valuable lessons.

Thank you for your insight into,
God's Word and His ways.
My life is richly 'Blessed'!

Thank you for your Faith,
And daily trust in God.
You have encouraged me.
To never stop believing,
In what God can do.

Thank you most of all,
For the unique blend of Love,
And understanding that makes,
Our relationship so special.

May God bless you,
And return to you in Abundance,
All the good things,
You have been faithful to share.

Happy Father's Day'!
Dad I Love you!
Lynelle Hodge (daughter), at age 17 yrs

Thanks

Thanks is a Way of returning our Love!
It is a Form of showing our Gratitude!
It is the Road of Acknowledgment!
And a Voice of Appreciation!
It is the walk of a smooth, peaceful, quiet path-way of
returning our Love,
A 'Love,' that is untouchable and unpredictable as the East is to the
West, and as the North is to the South.

It is a beautiful Form of showing our Gratitude,
Presenting an unforgettable perfume bouquet of sweet aroma of,
Multiple colours of flowers and roses, radiantly filling the atmosphere.

It is delightfully strolling the gratifying Road of Acknowledgment,
Meditating on the thoughtfulness and loving-kindness of a true heart.

It is the dramatic unforgettable, thrilling and irresistible Voice of Appreciation,
Echoing the harmonious rhythm, the anthem of joy and gladness.

It is the constant flowing of: sweet, warm, fresh, pure honey coming from the honey comb itself!
Thanks! Thanks! Thanks!

Thanks.

Thanks

It is Costless and Priceless,

It's 'Worth,' surpasses Silver and Gold,
Included Emerald, Diamond, Pearls and every Precious Stones.

It is a 'Light.'
It 'Lits our Face and Warms our Hearts,'
It reflects like a Mirror and shone like lights that never goes dim.

It is a 'River,'
It 'Overflows,' it Banks, the Bank of Tears,
'Tears,' of endless Joys and never ending Gladness.

It is an 'Energizer,'
Like God's energizing sun that always shines, and a thougher-bred-horse that never seems weary.
It energizes one's spirit positively throughout Life.

It is 'Powerful,'

Which depicts the dynamic unity of two super-powers,
Picturing the presence of an atomic-time-bomb awaiting to ignite.
Thanks.

THANKS! THANKS! THANKS!

THANKS! THANKS!

THANKS!

THANKS!
   Before you continue to read this, just raise both hands to heaven, and for a moment give God a shout of 'Thanks and Praise,' from the depth of your heart. Knowing He alone is worthy of this salute.
   Give thanks, to God first, then to all fellow men.
   In growing up at an early age, I discovered that God has blessed me, my other four sisters and three brothers with a God blessed mother, one who feared God, who taught us the Word of God from a very early age.
   Later years in life, looking back it was satisfying for me to see all what she has done for all eight of us, the wonderful example she set for us to imitates her as she read the Word of God, using it as her guide in training us and listening to God the Holy Spirit for our building and instructions. As I reminisce as far as I can, finding a word or phrases describing our 'God fearing Loving mother,' it was quite difficult because searching; Oxford's, Collins, Urban and Webster Dictionaries, in conclusion it almost seems impossible. Therefore, the only phrase that fits her well for a mother who spend countless hours in prayer and fasting, taking us daily in the presence of God on bended knees, crying out to God and loudly calling our names in prayer, I finally saw her as an angle. This helps me with the best phrase describing her as 'An Angel of Love Send from Heaven Above.' Prayers never dies, they are forever powerfully fresh and greatly affective!
   Among some of the everyday things she taught us, were "thank you," "I'm sorry," and "please." She also taught us to love the Lord and all men. These, along with other ethics, easily became part of

26

our everyday language and made it quite easy for us to say when there was a need.

We were practically taught to "give thanks to God," when we awake, throughout the day, and when we retired from our daily task before going to bed. What I am saying in simple language is. Our dear loving mother practically trained us to have morning devotions when we awake and evening devotion just before going to bed. So we had devotion twice daily!

Thanks became our everyday vocabulary, our daily practical exercise, our song and chorus and our best friend and slogan throughout our lives.

Our thanks to God and to all men while growing up, I believe should be something typifying this man in this short story.
In this short story, there are four characters.
Jerry, is the Boss and the employer who is white.
George, is the employee who is black.
Roy, is the highly respected man in the community.
Ethel, is the wife of Roy.

In growing up, I knew of this as a true story of a man in the village, where I once lived, whom I called George, who was employed by Jerry his Boss.

George grew up very respectful and always displayed great respect to all he came in contact with.

Each time Jerry speaks to George, in replying George always answers, No Sir! Or Yes Sir! This became a habit which greatly disturbed Jerry.

Jerry choose to have an emergency meeting with George before getting upset.
Jerry: George, can I see you in my office?

George: Yes Sir!

Jerry: George I am aware of the respect you have for me, but try stop saying. Sir! Sir! Sir! So often, because I do not like the constant reputation of it.

George replied, Yes Sir!

Jerry: (shouted in anger) George I do not like it! Would you stop saying it!

George: replied, Yes Sir!

Jerry: What else can I do or say in order for you to stop saying, Sir! Sir! Sir!

George: replied, I do not know Sir!

Jerry: Goodness gracious (stamping his feet) I have to do something about this!

Jerry took his case to Roy who is highly respected in the neighbourhood. A specialist in solving endless problems in the neighbourhood. Jerry: Roy I have a very serious problem with George!

Roy: replied, what am I hearing? George! No! Not George! This is unusual of him! George always bears a very good name; he is a very respectful person!

Jerry: This is my problem with him!

Roy: What! What! What! I do not understand!

Jerry: Yes! His respect is over and about too much for me!

Roy: I do not understand; explain to me in slow motion!

Jerry: I am aware of the respect George has for me as his employer, but I do not like his constant reply to me, each time I speak to him. He always replies Yes Sir! Or No Sir! This Sir! Sir! Sir thing irritates me and I am totally fed-up with it!

Roy: Ok! Now I understand what you are saying, and where you are coming from. Yes! Yes! Yes! I'll see what I can do, but this I have to handle very carefully and with great respect!

Jerry: Please do! I'll be very happy feeling much at ease. Thank you Roy!

Roy went home that evening, confused, not knowing how to handle this unusual hard to solve problem. What to say to George and trying to convert him into a new system. Roy final went to sleep!

Roy: (Roy and his wife sleeping in the same bed, he final fell asleep and quickly started dreaming loudly (this was unusual, unlike Roy who do not speak in his sleep at all). His wife decided she have to hear this episode because it sounded interesting, so she listened on. Roy started saying, 'This white man, what he want George to say to him? Yes Sir! No Sir! Is the correct thing to say in any reply in respect to any question asked! I can't understand, but Sir! Sir! Sir! (Roy stopped dreaming and fell asleep).

In the morning at the breakfast table, Ethel (his wife) closely keeping a keen eye on him, realized he ate little or no breakfast at all. So she decided to question his unusual appetite behaviour.

Ethel: Roy dear, are you feeling sick?

Roy: No! I am fine!

Ethel: Then what is it on your mind?

Roy: On my mind! Nothing!

Ethel: Ok! What were you dreaming about last night?

Roy: I dream! I don't dream! Like what?

Ethel: Who is this white man you have this problem with? Telling George to stop saying, No Sir! And Yes Sir! This Sir! Sir! Sir problem!

Roy: (laughed out loud), you mean to say this thing press me so much, I really dream about it? This white man (Jerry is George Boss), want me to deal with this case with George. He said, each time he speak to George, he kept replying to him, saying, No Sir! Yes Sir! This Sir! Sir! Sir thing! And he do not like the constant reply from George, who kept on repeating this Sir! Sir Thing!

Ethel (in the kitchen about to fry some eggs, the frying-pan sizzling hot). Raised her voice shouting in anger at Roy, saying, what non-sense you telling me? What he want George to say to him? No Sir! Yes Sir! Is the correct thing to say!

Roy: Well, since his Boss do not like to hear it so often, try to cut down on it!

Ethel: Cut down on what! What should George say, when a question is directed to him? He must make an answer and the answer remained the same, Yes Sir or No Sir! What else is there to say?

Roy: All I will tell him is, when you come to work in the morning, say, 'Good morning Sir' and when you fish working say, 'Good evening Sir'!

Ethel: Grabbed her hot frying pan, in an angry motion, wheeling it like a flying Helicopter at Roy, saying, I feel like baking your face instead of the eggs!

Roy: Seeing the angry motion of the red hot frying pan, like a Helicopter about to land on his head, trying to move, accidently his Alligator Boots slid and he found himself flat on his back, under the dining room table.

Ethel: replied, you Notting but a table rat!

Roy: replies, on his back, well! I! I! I try and George like a car stick in gear and can't get out, kept on saying, No Sir! Yes Sir! Sir! Sir! Sir!

Ethel: You better get out of this house today and go to work you know, before I find the priest and reverse did vow I make to you!

Roy: For peace sake, I gone!

Roy went all around looking for Jerry the Boss, found him eating his breakfast.

Jerry: greeted Roy with a smile, expecting he came to an agreed settlement. Jerry said, I know you have good news for me!

Roy: Replied and said, Jerry, I've tried my auto most and sad to say, but I have FAILED!

THIS IS WHAT GOD EXPECTS OF US, IN GIVING HIM THANKS.

This is what God expects of us (all humans), in our responds to Him as we live day by day and throughout our lives in giving Him thanks for all what He has done for us, all what He is doing and for all He promised to do for us for the future. He expects us to sound like George, constantly like a car stick in gear or record player, repeating ourselves in giving Him thanks.

Thanks to God should be the first and last word out of our mouths at the beginning and at the end of each day God 'Blessed' us with.

Thankfulness is gratitude to God for the blessings He bestows on us, in the past, present and the future. Why future blessings, because He is the only omnipotent, omnipresence and omniscience one. There is none like Him.

So many have failed and are still failing without noticing or realizing the danger of not saying thanks to God and to our fellowmen. This is a true sign of danger for us, our children and our future generations.

We need to stop, look, and listen to ourselves, urgently respond and address this out of control matter.

Why? Because, God is listening and waiting to hear from us, from the bottom of our hearts, words of Gratitude, Acknowledgements, Appreciations and Love which is thanks.

Today, mankind are so unthankful to God that our children are doing likewise. Let us be reminded that children are imitators of their parents.

A few years ago, when my son (Tristan) was about two and a half years of age (he is now is thirty-three), he was sick with a fever. His mother (Nurse) on duty at night, so I had to do the best I can for his relief. I tried giving him a baby aspirin tablet, and everything I knew possible in helping him, but to no avail. Finally, in using the wisdom that is on loan to me from God, I placed the baby aspirin tablet on my tongue while he was eager looking on, took some water then finally swallowed, he laughed in respond. Then he finally opened his mouth, as I placed the baby aspirin on his tongue, gave him some water and he gladly swallowed it. What he did was an imitation of his dad's action.

Imitation is a very powerful weapon, so we have to be very careful what we pass on to our children.

Un-thankfulness to God is a wrong and negative signal we are passing on to our children and God is unhappy with us, seeing us setting bad examples leading our children astray.

Thanks for many today, it is an 'Unknown Language,' to them it is a new vocabulary of which they have never heard of before. To some it is a 'Swearword,' to them it is a form of breaking the law. To others it is a 'Distasteful Medication,' something bitter and none appreciated by their taste buds. To a few the 'Road of Death,' a child will choose to be spanked to death, before saying, 'Thanks you'!

One may asked, to whom should I give thanks to? Thanks in every case should first be given to God, then out fellowmen.

Let us assumed you prayed to God asking Him for a new 'Car,' then three days later, a long-time school friend thought of you, knowing the condition of your 'Car,' then generously surprises you with a new car on your 'Birthday.' Whom are you going to give thanks to for the new 'Car,' which were given to you by an old long-time school friend? Your thanks should be first directed to God, then your school friend. Why? Simple, God is the one who is in full control of everything and has the power, to speak to people in numerous ways concerning doing a lot of things. In this case, remember God were first contact on blessing you with a 'Car,' then He spoke to your friend, through the power of God the Holy Spirit, about your need, and gave her the will to respond generously, showing kindness and love, presented you with this new 'Car.' Then secondly, turn to you generous old school friend saying, 'Thank you' for you timely generous 'Birthday Gift'!

The Psalmist David, is here telling us who deserves our first 'Thanks and Praise,' in all that we've been blessed with in life. He said, our 'Thanks and Praise,' should be directed to, our Lord God. Psalm 117, reads, 'O Praise the Lord, ALL YE NATIONS: praise Him, ALL YE PEOPLE.' For His merciful kindness towards us: and the truth of the Lord endureth forever. Praise ye the Lord.'

In Psalm 118:1, David reminds us to continue giving thanks to Our Lord God. "O, give thanks unto the Lord; for He is Good: because His Mercy endureth forever."

The Psalmist here reminding us to give thanks unto the Lord, and for the goodness of Him towards us as mankind.

God's Goodness is unchangeable to us, although we are all unworthy. His Goodness, surpasses all the; wisdom, knowledge and understanding of all mankind.

Next, the Psalmist says to give Him thanks for His Mercy, because His mercy is everlasting, which has neither beginning nor end and it is boundless.

In Isaiah 54:7, God's mercy is described as "sure." Peter describes God's mercy in 1 Peter 1:3 as "abundant." David also described God's mercy in Psalm 25:6 as "tender." In Lamentation 3:22–23, God's mercy is described as, "ever alive" and "never grows old." It is "new every morning!"

The Psalmist is reminding us to give thanks to God for His Mercy!

As we continue to give God thanks, what are some of the things we need to give thanks for?

We need to give God thanks for all His blessings towards us, both the visible and invisible blessings He gave us. We have been blessed in so many ways, with things we are unaware of. At times in life our blessings are so many, too numerous to count, even if we try we would surely fail, because as human we tend to forget, so we need to use this old lady new scientific 'Formula' when counting our 'Blessings.'

This old lady in trying to count her blessings, in giving God thanks, she realized they are so many and cannot be counted, so she decided to use her own 'Formula,' making sure all were collected and properly counted. So she decided to use the 'Weight and scale of Faith' Formula. So she gathered them all up together by 'Faith,' put them in her, 'Weight and scale of Faith,' and weigh them ton by ton, all the wonderful things that God has done for her. This is a wonderful idea, so I suppose we can use her 'Formula,' when giving God thanks for all the wonderful and great blessing, both seen and unseen, he bestowed upon us throughout our life.

As we continue to give God thanks, there are so many thing to give Him thanks for writing down and trying to remember everyone will be impossible for any human being . . . therefore let us look at a few.

Each created day He blessed us with, is precious, because it is a new brand day that will never be repeated again in the history of life . . . Give thanks!

Each day God created will always be remembered, because it will be recorded as history . . . Give thanks!

Each day God blessed us with life to see and to enjoy His great creation . . . Give thanks!

Each day is unique and most special, some people never lived to enjoy the full 24 hours, some lives were cut short by so many things too numerous to mention, but ours were saved. Give thanks!

Each day God blessed us with New Mercy. Give thanks!

Each day nature tells us that there is someone bigger that man, in full operation and He is God . . . Give thanks!

The Psalmist reminds us of God blessed days, saying, stop worrying about tomorrow and be happy today. Psalm 118:24 reads, "This is the day that the Lord hath made, let us rejoice and be glad in it." Give thanks!

Harry, Jane, Rudolph, Karen, Simon, Laverne, Terrance, and Maureen are all guilty of not giving God enough thanks!

What is the ratio of men giving God thanks today? Is it ten, twenty, or thirty percent? What is your answer?

Whatever it is, God is not happy! He is still passionately, lovingly, and earnestly asking, "Where are the other ninety percent of my unconditionally loving people?"

Where are the rest?

In this passage, we are going to see the displaying and operation of Jesus' mercy for man. Also, we are going to see the unthankfulness of man to God the Father, God the Son, God the Holy Spirit and the concluding results thereof. In conclusion, Jesus asks, in His loving-kindness, a very important question of man. He displays His unconditional love by gently asking, "Where are the rest?"

This question is one of the oldest ever asked. First, by God in the Garden of Eden ("Adam, where art thou?") and down through the ages until the very end of life. Moments before His Soon Second Coming to Earth, He will ask, "Where are the rest?"

From that time, all through the ages, His mercy and loving kindness continued.

Then in Samaria ten men experienced the operation of God's tender Mercy, but only one returned to say 'Thank you Jesus'! Again Jesus' 'Unconditional Love' and tender Mercy went on display, when He asked. Where are the nine or where are the rest?

This question first started in the beginning, in the Garden of Eden and continued throughout the ages, in Samaria of Galilee, presently now and it will continues until Jesus returned to this earth during the 'Rapture.'

In the Gospel of St. Luke: 17, reads, Jesus on one of His journey to Jerusalem, He passed through the middle of Samaria and Galilee.

Samaria was a city populated with foreigners of all different; creed, colour, nationality, language and culture. Also it was the place where people practise worshipping strange gods and idols, gods and idols of the different heritage and cultures. Also it was a place where false prophets inhabited, but was destroyed by God through His Prophet Elijah, during the time of proving who is the real true and living God? When Elijah, prayed and the true and living God responded with fire from on high destroying the sacrifice that was set on the altar Elijah build. It was also described or referred to, 'Crown of Pride,' people in this area allowed pride to controlled and rule their lives. It was a place where people lived a life of 'Un-thankfulness,' both to God and to man.

In the Gospel of St. Luke: 17 vs; 11- 19, reads, ' And it came to pass, as he went to Jerusalem, that he passed through the midst of Samaria and Galilee.

[12] And as he entered into a certain village, there met him ten men that were lepers, which stood afar off:

[13] And they lifted up their voices, and said, Jesus, Master, have mercy on us.

[14] And when he saw them, he said unto them, Go shew yourselves unto the priests. And it came to pass, that, as they went, they were cleansed.

[15] And one of them, when he saw that he was healed, turned back, and with a loud voice glorified God,

[16] And fell down on his face at his feet, giving him thanks: and he was a Samaritan.

[17] And Jesus answering said, Were there not ten cleansed? but where are the nine?

[18] There are not found that returned to give glory to God, save this stranger.

[19] And he said unto him, Arise, go thy way: thy faith hath made thee whole.

Jesus on one of his earthly ministry journey, entered a certain village, which is situated in the middle of the City of Samaria and Galilee, there He was confronted by ten men who were 'Lepers.' In those days 'Leprosy' which is similar to 'Ebola' and Aids today, it was a deadly disease with little or no cure in those days, so these people were, isolated and were cast out of the city, which cause them to be living in an area by themselves, because with this disease no one wanted to contaminated or to be put on death-row. They were counted to be unclean, and will have a bell or some mechanism attached to their bodies, that when they moved around, this sound indicated to the public that they are 'Lepers' (Unclean). I believed they heard a lot about Jesus, as He travelled around with this multitude flowering Him as He ministered the Word of God, performing great miracles; healing sick-folks, raising the dead and restoring people back to normal life. These ten 'Lepers,' were privileged and most happy to meet Jesus, having a face to face encounter with the 'Master' Himself.

Today people we are a most privilege people to have great opportunities still offered to us. Privileges to have the Word of God, presenting to us in so many ways, we can read it for ourselves and hearing it preached from pulpits endless of times. Telling us about the plan of Salvation and how we can be saved from the awful wrath and punishment of God and to be ready for Jesus' second return. These ten 'Lepers' too were privilege to meet Jesus face to face and wisely wasted no time but made good use this their 'Last chance of golden opportunity.' Can we learn a simple lesson from these ten sick Lepers, who used wisdom that they can continue living? Yes, they were wise! Those 'Lepers' were people like us, the used their last chance, as they walked their final mile. Jesus is coming we are walking our final mile, Jesus is extending His hand of 'Mercy to us and we are bluntly refusing His offer of Salvation. Simply take a leaf out of the 'Lepers,' book, give your heart to Jesus and like those 'Lepers,' continue living. Remember Jesus is offering us 'Eternal Life,' a life which has no end. John 3:16, reads, "For God so loved the world, that He gave His only begotten Son, that whosoever belieeveth in Him should not perish, but have everlasting life."

Today, we are a privilege people, who can come face to face with Jesus, tell him about our; aches, pains and hopelessness of life without Him. He is patiently and eagerly waiting to hear from us. He is the only hope of man, with plenty of 'Tender Loving Mercy,' awaiting us. Do like these ten 'Lepers,' shout or cry out to Him, asks for His help, He will never refuse. Forget about your pride, of the presence of your friends and loves ones. Confess your sins to Him, gladly open your heart's door and let Him in. Now! Why now? Next hour might be too late, just look around and see what is taking place as mankind walking the last mile of their road or life' journey and are not aware of it. Be obedient then you can fall prostate at Jesus' feet, having a threshing floor experience of giving Him thanks!

These ten 'Lepers,' when they say Jesus, the eyes popped opened, shining like a bright diamond star, when they behold the 'Master of Mercy,' Himself standing face to face.

They lifted up their voices; shouted, screamed, turned up their volume, to the maximum, crying in agony and pain caring not who were present, because this was their last chance and only hope of for their cure. Unashamedly they cried tears of bitterness, they shouted with a lamenting cry, 'Jesus'! What a wonderful name, what a beautiful name, none other name but the name of 'Jesus.' Jesus! Jesus! Trustful, hopeful, precious Jesus, something always happened when we call His Powerful Name (JESUS)!

These 'Lepers,' cried to the top of their voices, 'Jesus Master have Mercy on us'! At what time or point in life man chooses to cry to the top of His voice to Jesus begging Him to have Mercy on him? When we have tried everything and everything fail, this is the time man chose to call on Jesus to have or show Mercy. When the Doctor say, there is no hope, your illness, exceeds medical reach and help. When everyone turns their backs on us, such as family, friends and love ones. When trapped in an accident and no one to help. When trapped in a burning building on fire, face to face with death and no way of escaping. When a financial crisis arises, no one to help, just listening to the thundering of our hearts beat. When we find ourselves with our backs against the wall, surrounded by the enemy, the red sea before us and the only thing left is the 'MIRACLE MERCY OF GOD'!

Let us remember that God's Mercy is forever sure, forever great, forever abundant, forever tender and forever new every morning.

These 'Lepers,' cried to Jesus to show His Mercy, because the only Mercy they needed was that of Jesus and none other.

Did Jesus responded to their cry? Yes! Jesus responded with His Kind, Tender and Loving Mercy ('In Loving kindness, Jesus came my soul in Mercy to reclaim').

Jesus heard their cries of Mercy, then seeing their condition of their needs of His Mercy; He gave them a command, which they gladly obeyed. Obediently as they went and showed themselves to the Priest, 'THEY DISCOVERED THAT THEY HAVE 'ALREADY,' RECEAVED, THE MIRACLEOUS CLEANSING POWER OF JESUS' HEALING MERCY.' Jesus immediately healed them, but send them to the Priest proving their obedience to his command . . . but the work was already done. In those days the Priest were the ones responsible to perform these miracles. This is the reason He send them to the Priest, for him to witness their miracle.

When these ten 'Lepers,' saw and experienced 'The Miraculous Cleansing Power of Jesus' Healing Mercy.' What was their respond?

Did they turned back and give Jesus thanks?

Did they turned back to show their Gratitude to Jesus?

Did they turned back to show their Appreciation to Jesus?

Did they turned back with words of Acknowledgement to Jesus?

Did they turned back to show their Love to Jesus?

What is man's attitude and respond to Jesus when received His touch of Mercy? In responding to Jesus' Mercy, only one (a stranger) of the ten 'Lepers,' returned to give Jesus thanks!

Only one (a stranger) of the ten lepers, when He saw that he was healed and perfectly cleansed of his deadly incurable disease sickness, turned back, like a launching rocket, shouting, screaming, and crying to the top of his voice like a madman, Glorifying God. He was showing Jesus his gratefulness, appreciation, acknowledgement, and love, and giving him thanks for healing him. God is still looking for thankful worshippers today, giving Him thanks and showing some gratitude for all He has done, doing and promise to do!

The Psalmist in responding to God's Mercy in Psalm 4:7, which said, "Thou hast put 'Gladness' in my heart, more than in the time that their corn and wine increased." This is what I call "joy unspeakable and full of glory."

This stranger (one leper) not only did he glorified God, but humbled himself went way down, flat on his face, hitting the threshing floor, in tears of joy and gladness, at Jesus' feet, giving him thanks!

This is what God expects of us, in giving Him thanks for all what He has done, doing and promised to do for us.

Are we ready to 'Thank,' God the Father, God the Son, God the Holy Spirit for respond to all our cries?

Are we ready to thank Our Lord God, declare and decrees, commanding our ears, eyes, mouth, hearts, hands, feet, body, intellect, and our surroundings to give thanks and praise the Lord?

Are we ready to do like this 'Leper,' to have the threshing floor experience and the results thereof?

On the threshing floor is the only place we can hear, and receives clearly from God. On the threshing floor, God sees out heartaches, pains, tears and troubled. Also it is there prostate at His feet God understands all our inexpressible languages and prayers, as we reaches out to Him, for His Mercy and giving of thanks.

At times in life, when God answers our prayers, we feel so over-whelmed, that nothing can stop us from shouting to the top of our voices; in church, at work, in our homes, in the neighbourhood, on the streets, in the office, on the field of sports and in the Bank, in giving Him thanks and praise for what He has done for us . . . Give thanks to God, because He is worthy to be praise forever!

One hymn expresses these words, Only those who have an inti-mate relationship with God, knows how to truly express themselves in praising Him. And no one can say how much one should praise Him, because no one knows the wonderful and great things God has done for that person. It is a form of expression of joy, either; jumping and shouting His Name, lamenting tears of joy, dancing for a period of time, or just running around in a circle for a while. It is an expres-sion of the heart and a language only God understand. Most of the times this will take place at church, during the preaching session, when the preached Word touches their hearts relating to the blessings of God on their life. The Spirit of God moves, touching their hearts and this is the responding results.

At an ice-cold, freezing church, sad to say, where the Spirit of God is been quenched, denied or driven away, the Pastor will call for the security and give order to take them outside or in a different room. Saying they are disturbing the service; man traditional form of how should a service begins and ends, no time for the Spirit of God doing His Work and taking full controls. It is time for a change in a large percentage of churches today. Putting an end to; tradition, com-petition and man-pleasers doctrinal formula setting. Jesus is coming and people needs to hear the true preaching of the 'Gospel,' which is the good news of Salvation. Pastors it is time to preach telling the people the truth, because without the truth they will all end up in Hell, which is prepared for Satan and his fallen angels! All mankind was born in sin, having a sinful nature; there is punishment for sin, but there is also a remedy (The Blood of Jesus, which has the POWER to wash all sins away). Your congregation need to know; God love them, Jesus died for all their sins, paid the price for all men, Salvation is free (Some Churches today are chasing people away, because they are focusing and asking for too much MONEY), people needs to know there is; a God and a Satan and they are real, a Heaven and a Hell, eternal-life and eternal-damnation, Jesus is coming soon and they needs to get ready and be prepared to meets Him in the Rapture. If they failed to accepts Him as their Saviour, them the result is punishment in 'Hell'! Let them know He is Merciful, loving and kind, waiting to show them His Mercy, as He did to these 'Ten Lepers,' in the City of Samaria of Galilee.

After Jesus, received that threshing floor heartfelt thanks from the only leper in His Tender, Loving Mercy, Jesus turned to him and asked him two questions. Were there not ten cleansed? Then where are the nine or where the rest, to give thanks?

Today Jesus is asking this same question, that God asked thousands of years ago, as He did in the Garden of Eden. As He looked down from heaven above, seeing the few men, women and children out at church giving Him thanks each Sunday.

In spite of our unthankfulness and attitude to Him, in His Unconditional Love, and Tender Mercy, He continues to ask. Where are the nine? Or where are the rest?

Where are the nine or where are the rest? This is referring to; our children's, other family members, neighbours, bosses, co-workers and friends. Also those whom Jesus; healed from their sickness, rescued, protected, delivered. Those who were set free from; accidents, house-fire, drifting boats on stormy seas, prisons, financial problems, hurricanes, wars and various forms of life. All who continues receives the daily blessings of God, the rain He blesses us with and the whole volume of the blessings of life, nature and the full works of His creation.

Those who once ran well and dropped out of the race. All the Nations and entire world-population who forgets God. Psalm 117:1, reads, "O Praise the Lord, ALL YE NATIONS: praise Him, ALL YE PEOPLE. For His merciful kindness towards us: and the truth of the Lord endureth forever. Praise ye the Lord."

Unthankfulness and pride filled the hearts, and lives of the remaining nine 'Lepers,' who refused to return in giving thanks to Jesus.

Are we aware of the gross insult when failing to say thanks to man? How much more God feels when we refused to say, 'Thank you Lord'?

Jesus said, they are not found to return to give glory to God, save one stranger.

Today God is still asking the same question. Where are the nine or where are the rest? Are we ready to return giving God thanks?

Next Sunday, let us all try to encourage as much as we can of that, 'Nine, which is 90%, of the Rest,' having our Churches full and overflowing?

Let us give thanks to Our Lord God, with our hearts full of gratitude, appreciation, acknowledgement, and love, because He is 'Worthy'! Give thanks!

In giving thanks to God, we are going to hear the same words that Jesus spoke to the only leper, "Arise stand up, get up from the threshing floor, your prayer is answered! Go thy way; thy faith hath made thee whole!" Peace and Joy forevermore, words that only Jesus alone can speak.

From the cradle to the grave, all men need to give God thanks! Give God thanks! Give God thanks! Give God thanks!

Ten "lepers" were healed, cleansed, and made whole, but only one returned to give thanks. Jesus was, and is still, unhappy with our lack of acknowledgement, appreciation, gratitude, and love for all what He has done, is doing, and promised to do for us.

People give thanks! Give thanks! GIVE THANKS TO GOD! PEOPLE GIVE THANKS TO GOD!
COUNTRY GIVE THANKS TO GOD!
NATIONS GIVE THANKS TO GOD!
WORLD GIVE THANKS TO GOD!

People take heed to God's warning voice. Prepare get ready Jesus is coming soon!

We are living in the last and closing days as the word of God teaches, we are constantly hardening our hearts, and dismissing Him from our thoughts and hearts. The bells of His coming are constantly ringing, "Jesus is coming, get ready, prepare to meet the King of Kings and Lord of all Lords." Are you ready? Repent while there is life! Get ready NOW!

Starting January 2012 and continuing, we are seeing more and more evidence of the Lord's coming. Some of these signs are; deaths of thousands of birds. Some of them are said to have broken backs, and from reports, the best scientists cannot explain these strange happenings. This is a serious sign and if this should continue, it would be fair to say that there would be a shortage of poultry around the world.

Additionally, thousands of dead fish, and mammals, have washed up on the sea shores. This phenomenon will also add to the existing threat of food shortage.

In one of my dreams, the Lord showed me a sign of the seas turning jet black. If the seas turn black, life in the sea will surely die. If all life which gives food to man disappears, quite naturally there will be a shortage of meat and fish for human consumption. Is this a plague, a curse, a signal of the coming of King Jesus? The answer is, yes! This sadly will plunge the world into great famine. People

Jesus is coming again get ready and prepare to meet the Saviour of the World.

Another sign is the mysterious dying of animals especially the cattle. This will bring another shortage of meat, milk, butter, cheese and the list goes on.

People get ready Jesus is coming, escape the wrath of God to come. John: 3:16, states, "For God so loved the world, that he gave his only begotten son, that whosoever believeth in him, should not perish, but have everlasting life." Salvation is free; Jesus has already paid the price for our sins over 2000 years ago on the cross of Calvary. He cried it is finished; man's redemption has been paid because of His unconditional love for all men.

The bees have also vanished, to where, no one seems to know. Bees are very important to the sustenance of life because they play a very crucial role in the pollination of plants. If bees disappear for a long while, this can cause a great threat to a shortage of food. It is said, although a few bees are still around, scientists have discovered that the queen bees are not returning to the bee-hive as they should. The queen bees have no control over their behaviour, the creator is in control. This is another sign of the soon return of the Son of God, the Lord Jesus Christ.

We are entering into a serious season of great famine and governments around the world are not responding to the conditions of the day. The Bible reminds us of the importance of visionaries, it said, where there is no vision the people will perish.

We are in the midst of a series of signs and wonders and only a few people are really concerned about these strange patterns. There are also visitations of strange objects in the earth's zone, both appearing and disappearing without leaving any evidence and clue of their missions. Many have concluded that these visitations are actually aliens from other planets. How can this be when scientists have concluded that life forms on other planets are impossible? People God is; merciful, loving, kind, longsuffering and gracious to all mankind, and all these warnings are saying, "prepare now," because His return can be any moment believe it or not.

GIVE GOD THANK FOR HIS WRITTEN WORD

The Bible teaches us, how, when, where and why we ought to live our daily lives.

It tells us about our lives, even before we were born.

It teaches us spiritually; how, when, where and why we ought to eat in order to live a long and healthy life.

It tells us about our strength and weaknesses and how to balance life and be victorious.

It is a Hammer, it teaches us; how, when, where and why we need to use the Word of God, to break in pieces the speed bumps, road blocks and hindrances of Satan in our pathway of life.

It is a Lamp, which is a vessel that is filled with oil, this oil is a symbol of God the Holy Spirit. So it teaches us as children of God, how, when, where and why our vessels needs to be filled with God the Holy Spirit.

It is a Light, it simply teaches us, the importance of having our lives illuminated with the Light of the Word, guiding, shinning, glowing and living within us, who is Jesus Christ Our Lord. Why do we need the Light within us? To put out and expel the darkness from within us! How can one receive the Light? By opening our hearts door and let Jesus in! Who is the Light of the World? Jesus said, I am the Light of the World! Where is the Light? He is always present right next to you! When can one get the Light? Right now!

It is a Sword, a weapon of war. It teaches us the importance of knowing; how, when, where, and why the Word of God, ought to be used, as Jesus did when He was confronted by Satan in the wilderness after fasting for forty days and forty nights.

It also teaches us how to use the Word of God to stop, intersect, crush, and totally destroy the missiles of the enemy . . . which is Satan and his army.

It is a Mirror, as we look into it, we see a picture, a reprint and a reflection of ourselves from the cradle to the grave and far beyond the grave, that point to Jesus, our Eternal Hope.

So each day as we continue to live and enjoy the blessings of a new day that God created for us, let us continue to give God thanks, for the Bible (the written Word of God).

We tend to overlook in giving God thanks, as we pray. We overlook things like, the storms of life that aids our spiritual growth and helps us to grow stronger and say thank you to those thoughtful folks who find time and faithfully pray for us.

All Governments good or bad, pray that God gives them wisdom, helping everyone to make the right decisions . . . say a prayer, render not evil for evil and let God fix it. He said, be still and know that I am God!

Those who you consider an enemy, say a good prayer . . . God said, love them still, and remember vengeance is mine!

All neighbours, good or bad, love your neighbour, remember love conquerors everything!

The prophet obediently brought that prophetic Word, from God the Holy Spirit, changing your life completely.

All those men and women, who keep our streets clean, pray that God blessed them and their families in every areas of their life.

WE NEED TO GIVE GOD "THANKS" FOR THE INSPIRED WRITTEN WORD OF GOD: THE HOLY BIBLE.

The Bible teaches us, how, when, where and why we ought to live our daily lives.

It tells us about our lives, even before we were born.

It teaches us spiritually; how, when, where and why we ought to eat in order to live a general long, strong and healthy life.

It tells us about our; growth, strength, weaknesses, balance and the giant that is within us, spiritually, physically, financially, morally, mentally and how to be mighty victorious in all these areas of life.

It is a Hammer, it traches us; how, when, where and why we need to use the Word of God, to break in pieces the speed bumps, road blocks and hindrances of Satan in our pathway of life.

It is a Lamp, which is a vessel that is filled with oil, this oil is a symbol of God the Holy Spirit.

So it teaches us as children of God, how, when, where and why our vessels needs to be filled with God the Holy Spirit.

It is a Light, it simply teaches is, the imperativeness of having our lives illuminated with the Light of the World, guiding, shinning, glowing and living within us, who is Jesus Christ Our Lord.

Why do we need the Light within us? To put out and expels the darkness from within us!

How can one receive the Light? By opening our hearts door and let Jesus in!

Who is the Light of the World? Jesus said, I am the Light of the World!

Where is the Light? He is always present right next to you!

When can one get the Light? Right now!

It is a Sword, a weapon of war. It teaches us the imperativeness of knowing; how, when, where, and why Lifesaving weapon (sword), which is the Word of God, ought to be used, as Jesus did when He was confronted by Satan in the wilderness after fasting for forty days and forty nights.

It also teaches us how to use the Word of God strategically, to stop, intersects, crushes, defeats and totally destroys the missiles of the enemy . . . which is Satan and his army.

It is a Mirror, as we look into it, we see a picture, a reprint and a reflection of ourselves from the cradle to the grave and far beyond the grave, that point to Jesus, our Eternal Hope. And this plan was drawn up long before God created the world.

So each day, as we continue to live and enjoy the blessings that God created for us, let us continue to give God thanks for the Bible (the written Word of God).

Give God Thanks.

- For taking us from one point of destination to another.
- For giving us the strength to pick up our keys.
- For controlling our subconscious state of mind (sleeping).
- For kindhearted folks who voluntarily go that extra mile for a total stranger.
- For faithful preachers who deliver the Word of God.
- For earth on which we trod.
- For all the seasons of life.
- For all the talents and gifts that God lends us.
- For the human race with its varying culture and language.
- For all the insects that completed God's wonderful work of creation.

- For all those who born without hands, feet, eyes, and ears, but are operating just as well as those who were born with all their extremities.
- For all the blessings we received without asking of God.
- For all the miracles we experienced in life.
- For all the different species of birds and the different tunes and songs they sing.
- For the unique creation of languages and the understanding of each other, with help and training. This sounds like nothing but it is all God's Miracle!

Let us all remember to give God thanks for everything, because He is Worthy!

Olympians give God the glory, "Say Thanks!"

Olympics in China August, 2008.

Having just had the winding down of the Olympics in China, the country displayed to the rest of the world their latest technology and talents while the world enjoyed all the sporting events that was performed.

It was said that their presentations will be remembered as a historic mile stone in the hearts and minds of all who were present, as second to none.

News is now flashing that the next Olympic event in 2012, is going to be staged right here in Great Britain, London. When it is all finished, the State of the Art Stadium, preparations, celebrations and the whole works will surpass China's staging of Olympic, 2008, the bell has been wrung, the stage is set, and the whole world is eagerly watching with excitement to see the rumble of the first round between China and host country Great Britain.

As the Olympians achieve their medals, I found one thing lacking, more than 75% of the medallist give thanks to coaches, lovers, parent, Government, friends and well-wishers. They forget to give God the Glory for what He has done, what He is doing and all what he will continue to do. Hearing this saddened me. Olympians, who blessed you with Life to do your daily training? Where does your strength come from? The Psalmist reminds us that our Strength comes from the Lord.

I can vividly remember, 'The Queen of Lawn Tennis, Serena Williams,' on her last Australian tour, she acknowledged the presence and help of God, and I quote her 'want to give God Jehovah Thanks for all His help.'

Giving thanks is very important in every area of life. It should be our slogan and chorus throughout life's journeys. It is an expression of our heartfelt love; it is an answer to our prayers.

Remember, God is the Creator of everything, which means He is the Creator of sports as well. Sports are one of the few things that unite, bind and knit people of all walks of life together. This is what God wants and expects of us as human beings. God is happy when we are united with each other. Unity among mankind makes God laughs. Unity is; togetherness, strength, power and love.

God wants us to be happy and to enjoy life to its fullest. He also wants us to be excited, successful and victorious in every sport we passionately love, because He is a great lover of sports. He wants us to always do better that our best at all times when preforming at every level. He wants us to exceed our opponents and be victorious.

Remember the Apostle Peter, out-ran the other disciples on the way to the Tomb to ascertain if the tomb, the place where Jesus was buried was really empty, and he saw it was and still remains today. Jesus arose from the grave with all His Power, defeating death, as He defeated death, so Jesus wants us to defeat all our opponents. We cannot forget the Prophet Elijah, who out-ran King Ahab with his horses and chariots and beat them to their destination. God also wants us to outperform all other "stars," and to be the only Star among the rest. God expects us to imitate him; He wants us to be like Him. God is Champion of all Champions, so naturally He too wants us to be Champions as well.

BUSINESS MAN AND WOMAN GET READY, JESUS IS COMING.

On leaving school at age seventeen, I worked at a supermarket, earning some money to make a start in life. I was excited to commence this start; I got involved in the business and the new atmosphere.

At this small super market, there was a small staff, the boss and a cleaner. A woman I will refer to her as 'Pat,' and the owner Mark.

Mark was in his early sixties and wealthy. He had many friends, money, properties, vehicles, a wife and grown children all working and doing well. He was a quiet, cool, soft spoken, and smartly dressed individual. He wore a black, Texan Cow Boy hat, on the side of his head, at the corner of his mouth was a cigarette, which he smoked.

Pat the cleaner was a very loud, vocal person; she always had a broom in her hand, a rag over her shoulder and was always singing in a high octave voice. It was a pleasure for her to help anyone who had a problem.

Once I heard a conversation between Mark and Pat. Mark was sitting on his office steps, looking quite unhappy. Pat saw his facial expression, and tried to help as usual. Pat started the conversation:
Pat: Mark, what's the matter with you? You look sleepy. Didn't you get enough sleep last night?

Mark: No girl

Pat: Well then, what's your problem?

Mark: I can't sleep at all

Pat: Then what's going on?

Mark: in a low voice, almost in a whisper, every time I put my head down and close my eyes to sleep, all I can see is my money, properties and business in front of me and I can't sleep at all

Pat: Are you serious? This is terrible!

Mark: It's true, it's true.

Sadly, Mark died a few months later after that conversation.

Today there are many people all over the world, walking the streets, going to their jobs, doing business as usual, encountering this same experience, and are seeking ways of ending their lives.

People are constantly shutting God out of their lives. Living a life of self, worshipping their earthly achievements, and refusing to give God thanks, They have everything, with the exception of one thing—giving their hearts to God.

God is Love, and wants us to be happy and to enjoy all the wealth and riches which he provides for us.

Some people believe that being a Christian; one must be poor and downhill, Oh no! God wants us to eat the best meals, wear the finest clothes, drive the best vehicle and just live a happy life.

In conclusion remember to be obedient to God's command, love all men everywhere, ask Him for the key of Wisdom, because, 'Except the Lord build the house, they labour in vain that build it. And let all our lives have the stamp of approval and signature of the will of God.

Covenantly Blessed!

This is the Word of the LORD Himself!

St. Luke: 2, v. 23, reads, 'As is it written in the law of the LORD, EVERY MALE THAT OPENETH THE WOMB shall be called holy to the LORD.'

Cover and Blessed!

I am Blessed! I am Blessed! I am Blessed!
I am Blessed like Abraham, Isaac, Jacob, Jabez, Jesus, Job, John, Tristan, Landon, Kashief, Junior, Joseph and Vernelle Hodge, Pastor Gladstone Hazel, Prince Charles, Prince William, Prince George of Cambridge, Conrad and Kareem Kelly, James and Robert Simpson, I am Blessed!

I am Blessed, even before the world began, I am blessed!
I am blessed, like Jesus who is Wonderful, Counsellor, the Mighty God, The Everlasting Father, the Prince of Peace, I am Blessed!
I am blessed because it is written in the Law of the Lord, I am blessed!
I am covered and blessed, approved and signed by God long before I was born, I am blessed!

I am covered and blessed, as the First Male born to my mother, I am blessed!
I am covered and blessed, and holy to the Lord, I am blessed!

I am Cover and blessed, and extremely special unto the Lord, I am blessed!
I am covered and blessed, and most precious to the Lord, I am blessed!
I am covered and blessed, and unique to the Lord, I am blessed!
I am blessed! I am forever covered and blessed! I am Blessed!
I am blessed, each day of my entire life, I am blessed!

On October 19th, 2008, God once more with His stamp of approval graciously and wonderfully bestowed another measure of His Divine Blessing on our life. This was the birth of our first grandchild a baby boy (first male grandson), whose name is Landon Patrice Hodge, who according to God's Holy Word, bears a Life Covenants title as 'Holy to the Lord'!

Are you the first male born son of your mother? Like Jesus the first male born of Mary or Isaac the first born male of Sarah? If this is your position in your family, then get to know your real position in life in this world in which you live. Remember God's Word is true and truth stands forever and it is unchangeable.

In this world in which we live, we are all blessed, but there is a vast distinction between the first male, born of all mothers and the remaining males in all families. Again this is not my opinion or my words!

According to God's Holy Word, those of us, including myself, my son Tristan, and grandson Landon P Hodge, and all males that open their mother's womb, are according to God's Holy Word:
Covenantly, Holy to the Lord!
Covenantly, Special to the Lord!
Covenantly, Precious to the Lord!
Covenantly, Unique to the Lord!

All first born males are Covenantly blessed all the days of their lives.

If you are the first male of your mother and is President or former President of a country, the Prime Minister or former Prime Minister, Governor or former Governor, Doctor, Pilot, a Star, Specialist, Designer, Inventor, King, Cricketer, Footballer, Golfer, Tennis player,

Pastor, Professor, President of schools, universities, companies etc. You are blessed and blessed forever!

This is no mistake; this is the covenant blessings of God on your life. So let us collectively join our hearts and voice as we sing, over and over, "I am blessed!" This is a form of acknowledgement to God in giving Him thanks for His Covenant Blessing on all male who are born in this position in life.

This is no mistake; this is God's will, plan and purpose for us, long before the world began.

The Apostle Paul, in his address to a young preacher, teacher, and Pastor of a church in Crete said, "In hope of eternal life, which God, that cannot lie, promised before the world began" (Titus: 1:2).

If you are one of us, and still do not know for sure of your true position in this life, immediately get on the emergency line to God, call Him up, and talk to Him. He is waiting to hear from you, tell Him what you want and I know He will surely help you. That's the kind of God He is. Therefore, let us all continue to give Him Thanks, singing, I am blessed!

Warning! Warning!

The Prayer of Repentance and acceptance.

Jesus is coming back to this earth again, just as He promised, no one knows when, but it can be anytime. This message of climate change is God's final warning to mankind. This is the same final message God gave to Noah to the people before that final destruction.

If you do not know the Lord Jesus as your Saviour and you want to be prepared before He comes, simply say the prayer of repentance from your heart and be accepted into His Kingdom. Jesus said, we need to confess with our mouths and He will answer our prayers by forgiving us and receiving us into His Kingdom, where we will live eternally with Him.

The dying thief on the cross prayed a simple prayer, he said, "Lord remember me when thou comest into thy kingdom," then Jesus said unto him, "Verily I say unto thee. Today shalt thou be with me in paradise." You too can enter paradise by saying this prayer:

"Father, I come to you in Jesus precious name. Lord Jesus, I thank you for your presence, I know that I am a sinner and I believe that you died on the cross, shedding your precious blood for every sin which I have committed. I now open my heart and I ask you to come in and cleanse me from all my sins with your blood. Wash me, pardon me and accept me as I repent and live inside of me as I now choose to follow you. Thank you for saving me, be my Saviour, Lord and Friend in Jesus precious name Amen'.'

Take this prayer to your children and everyone you know. Do not go to heaven alone, take someone with you!

A TRIBUTE TO HER MAJESTY QUEEN ELIZABETH II

'God Save the Queen.' 29th October, 2010.

God save our gracious Queen!
Long live our noble Queen!
God save our Queen!
Send her victorious,
Happy and glorious,
Long to reign over us,
God Save the Queen!

God Bless you! Your Majesty Queen Elizabeth II, were born on the twenty first day of April, nineteen hundred and twenty six (1926). You were blessed, long before you were born. Long before the world began. God specifically hand-picked you according to His; will, plan and purpose for this time, for this season and for this era, because He is God.

In Titus 1:2, the Apostle Paul wrote to his young preacher, Titus, saying, "In hope of eternal life, which God, that cannot lie, promised before the world began." Long before the world began, in God's plan, you were purposefully chosen to reign as Queen. God's Word is true, He keepeth His promise forever and He is a God that cannot lie! God's plans and purposes must be fulfilled before His return. In the Book of Isaiah 55:11, He said, "So shall my word be that goeth forth out of my mouth: It shall not return unto me void, but it shall accomplished that which I please, and it shall prosper in the thing whereto I sent it."

This is a tribute to you, Your Majesty Queen Elizabeth II. You are beautiful, quiet, soft-spoken, generous, multi-talented, multi-gifted, multi-skilful, loving, peace-maker, who is kind-hearted, pride-taker, calm, thankful, humble and wise and forever a passionate and precious person, who is also full of praise and will openly worship God our Saviour. You who were born in the season of spring, a time when the roses always bloom and provide an atmosphere perfume with the aroma of sweet scented flowers. The bee's and birds sweetly singing, and the silky butterflies, flying, glowing in the golden sun across the blue glassy skies far above.

My name is John Adolphus Hodge, born on 21st April, 1954, to Mrs. Dolly Agatha Henrietta Hodge and Mr. Wilfred Adolphus Hodge. I was born on the beautiful island of St. Kitts, (Sweet Sugar City and the Land of Beauty of the entire Caribbean), Leeward Island, West Indies. I am a born-again, blood-bought, blood-washed child of the Most High God, and for this I give Thanks to God! I was blessed with two children; Lynelle and Tristan Hodge. Their mother Merle Hodge, also one grandson Landon Patrice Hodge. I am the third of eight blessed children, consisting of four girls and four boys. I love the Lord with all my heart and my purpose in life is to be obedient to Him in doing His will, as He daily speaks to me.

In the year 1961, my mother Mr. Dolly Hodge, whom were also born on 7th April, 1926, came to England to join our father and husband, who had both migrated to England three years previous. My father resided in UK, Birmingham, the city where he had lived and worked for many years. Mommy came to England leaving behind five children, Jean, Melvina, John, Joseph and Stanley Hodge. We were left in the care of a loving couple, who had no children of their own. I was that middle child of the five children left behind.

In 1964 our mother returned home, to the beautiful Island of St. Christopher/St. Kitts, West Indies, because of her love for us. 'Mommy' as we longingly and graciously delights in calling her, returned with two more children, Moses and Brenda and was expecting a third child, to be her last, our sister Esther.

I know questions are flooding your mind, Such as, why didn't she wait until the child was born? The answer to your question is this! We, who were left behind, were not well taken care of as promised. So our mother who loved us and whom we loved dearly, did not hesitate, spared no time, immediately packed and swiftly return to continue to care for her remaining five loving children. 'THANK YOU MOMMY'!

Today, I am very proud of our loving mother, and I pause to say, 'God Bless Our Mother'! I always referred to our mother as, 'An Angel of Love' sent from Heaven Above. Our mother closed her eyes on 8th February, 2004, God being well pleased with the work she had accomplished for Him. She had brought up and cared for eight children, and numerous untold men and women including the sick, the aged and lonely folks, gave their hearts to God, and were blessed as she ministered to their needs. I know of other mothers who stayed, but 'mommy' loving came to our rescue, and there isn't another mother in the WORLD like her!

When our mother returned home in 1964, she brought in her handbag, a little diary, which consist of a calendar, a list of historical events, dates of public holidays, and other important things. At that time, I was nine years old. I remembered I took that little pocket diary and started to read it and happily I made an historical discovery. While reading I discovered that Her Majesty Queen Elizabeth II, was born on 21st April, 1926. I then remembered running to mommy excitedly shouting and saying Mommy! Mommy! The Queen and I were born on the same date, (21st April).

My mother took the little pocket diary, examined it carefully to see if my discovery was correct. Then she affirmed I was right and it was also news to her as well. She herself had also failed to discover that both she and the Queen were born fourteen days apart. I had only recently made that discovery myself.

My mother was born on 7th April, 1926, while Her Majesty Queen Elizabeth II, being born on 21st April, 1926. Our mother truly portrays all those qualities identified earlier of Her Majesty.

As I continued to advance in years, especially my school days, I vividly remembered actively checking both in school, at church and where ever I travelled, checking to see who else were born on this very date. This became a fun activity but also stirred my curiosity and continued to do so to this day. So far I have discovered it to be a rare date and indeed continues to have a very low percentage birth-rate. On the 21st April, 2010, I made my 56th Birthday, I cannot recall counting ten people whom were born on this rare date.

Her Majesty Queen Elizabeth II, as I grow and mature as a Christian, I continued to pray for you and never cease praying for you, simply because I truly consider you to be very 'Special,' from the day of my discovery of your date of birth.

Today I can say without a shadow of doubt, 'you are greatly blessed,' and that Blessings from above' will never depart from you. You are blessed, with good health, wealth, long life and indeed his list has no end in sight. I cannot think of anyone else in this world, who continues to be carried along, on this sea of excellence and in an atmosphere of life-long BLESSINGS.

My Bible teaches me about the power of the tongue. It teaches me that there is life and death in 'the power of the tongue.' Our tongue is small but yet a very powerful. God showed us by practical demonstration, in the third verse in the Bible. God by the power of His tongue, He created something out of nothing. With the power of His tongue, God said, "LET THERE BE LIGHT, AND THERE WAS LIGHT!" God has blessed us with a tongue, which is the organ of speech, and can be used for good and evil.

Our tongue is a weapon and a missile which can destroy. It is also an instrument that can lightened our burden, bright our faces and warm our hearts. It can be destructive as fire, destroying everything in its path and beyond. It is so powerful it steers the course of life for any individual until death, where it will finally lay still and pow-erless. So as we us our tongue, let us all be careful of what we say.

Today, Your Majesty, in appreciation and gratitude, I say 'THANK YOU' to you, for all you've done for all the former Commonwealth Countries.

Since my birth until this day, all of the Commonwealth Countries, over the years all over the world, the commonwealth used their tongue and sing, the anthem, 'God save the Queen,' which is an anthem of prayer to God on your behalf. We open with God Save the Queen, we acknowledge your reign with, long to reign over us, and the closing line is, 'God Save the Queen'!

This is an 'Anthem of Prayer to God on your behalf.' The national anthem has been sung and still continues to be sung by millions of school-children and adults, on your behalf reaching the Throne of God. A prayer that God hears and honours, and the results of which are untold 'BLESSING'! You are blessed by the power of the tongue! You are blessed! You are blessed! You are blessed!

May God continue to shower you, your family and the royal household with His abundant Blessings, as the whole world continues daily to enjoy the splendour of His great creation.

Her Majesty Queen Elizabeth II, God loves you and so do I. May His Blessings forever be yours. I close with these four verses of scripture.

Proverbs: chapter 31 verses 25—28.

Strength and honour are her clothing; and she shall rejoice in time to come. She openeth her mouth with wisdom; and in her tongue is the Law of kindness. She looketh well to the ways of her household, and eateth not the bread of idleness. Her children arise up, and called her blessed; her husband also, and he praiseth her

HER MAJESTY, THE QUEEN DEMONSTRATED UNCONDITIONAL LOVE.

Northern Ireland, Unforgettable day of Unconditional-Love. Her Majesty, Queen Elizabeth II, displayed herself as a genuine person. She demonstrated forgiveness and purity of heart.

Few people often cannot express their opinion of Her Majesty because they are afraid to give an honest opinion of her. In God's written Holy Word, it says; people have eyes but they cannot see, ears but they cannot hear mouths and lips but speak confusing things, hearts but have vain desires. If God is not in the picture, what do we expect? Everything will be out of control and will make no sense. And this is why some people cannot give an honest opinion of the Queen who is of God's own heart!

Her Majesty is radiant and beautiful. The people of Northern Ireland and the whole world have been touched and moved by her amazing attitude. She is a positive role model and a great mentor. Your Majesty, Thank you! This is the Voice of God to the World . . . a message of peace. May God's blessings continue to protect, cover and lead you throughout your reign.

No one can pray to and praise the true and living God, with their hearts full of sin. First, we are to be sincere and righteous for God to hear and answer our prayers, this is what Her Majesty has done by obediently honoring God and His Word. Jesus said in Mark 11:26, "But if ye do not forgive, neither will your Father also which is in heaven forgive your trespasses." In 1 John 4:20, "If any man say, I love God, and hateth his brother, he is a liar; for he that loveth not his brother whom he hath seen, how can he love God whom he hath not seen?"

Hymn

"O for a heart to praise my God'.'

O for a heart to praise my God,
A heart from sin set free,
A heart that always feels the blood,
That freely shed for me.

A Heart of Love.

Is there any "Love," in our Hearts to quickly forgive?

Is there any "Love," in our Hearts to tenderly embrace our stubborn enemies?

Is there any "Love," in our Hearts to voluntarily give a true helping hand?

Is there any "Love," in our Hearts to gladly render good for evil?

Is there any 'Love,' in our Hearts to willingly and gladly show mercy?

Is there any "Love," in our Hearts to patiently reach-out to the needy?

Is there any "Love," in our Hearts truly for "All Men Everywhere" In spite of "Race, Colour, Language or Creed?

God who is "Love," has being offended by man,

Yet His "Love,' remains the same.

If we are followers of God, "Yes" we too can do likewise.

Love is a "Healer"; it has the Power to heal!

It has the Power to heal "ALL WOUNDS," which is caused by the hatred of man,

Love is the only conqueror, which conquerors everything that is applied to life and living!

People, God loves us "Unconditionally" it matters not what we've done and who we are, so let us all love one another!

God's Will and Plan for Prince William and Kate Middleton

Before Creation Began.

WILLIAM:
WILL = God's Word and choice is fulfilled!
I AM = I Am the only, I Am God!
KATE:
Kind and **K**nowledgeable, **A**ttractive and **A**ssured,
Tender-hearted and **T**rustworthy, **E**legant with full **E**ndurance.
Kind and **K**nowledgeable, including becoming his beautiful **'Princess'**!
Attractive and **A**ssured of capturing his heart, soul and mind,
By being the apple of his eyes and his only heart's desire!
Tender-hearted and **T**rustworthy, which exceeds and surpasses, the price of minerals, diamonds silver, gold and every precious stones!
Elegant with full **E**ndurance patiently, quietly and sacrificially waiting, knowing the price is right!

Kate, this is God's Will, Plan and Purpose for you in this life!
Long before the world began, I the Lord God of Host has chosen him!
His name is 'William,' he is my 'WILL' for you, take him!
I have provided, protected, preserved, and now presents him to you!
I AM the Lord God of Host, the Great I AM that has spoken!

He is forever covenantly-blessed by the Lord God of Host long before his birth!

Because he is the first male that opened the womb of his mother!

He is Unique, Special and Precious unto the Lord and to you as well!

I have chosen him for you, it's real all doubts are settled, signed and approved by God,

The only I AM!

William at age 28, kindly open the gate and graciously marry your; loving and Attractive Princess Kate!

Kate Dear, I 'Prince William,' will always and forever passionately love you!

I 'WILL,' Cherish, Protect, Honour and Adore you as long as we both live!

I William, 'WILL,' love you, as Christ loves the Church and gave Himself for it!

Knowing this is God's Plan, Purpose and Will for our lives before we were born!

Now may the blessings of God's promise, fruitfully multiplies and generates resulting in future generation to come!

We are Blessed! We are Blessed! We are forever Blessed!
We are Blessed! We are Blessed! We are forever Blessed!

GOD'S SIGNATURE AND APPROVAL OF PRINCE WILLIAM AND KATE MIDDLETON BOND OF LOVE.

Mr. John A Hodge
28 Church Drive
Carrington
Nottingham
NG5 2BA

12th February, 2011.

Prince William
C/O Her Majesty the Queen
Buckingham Palace
London
SW1 1AA.

Dear Prince William and Kate Middleton,

   Greetings in the wonderful name of the Lord Jesus Christ our Saviour, Redeemer and King; whose coming is nearer today than it was yesterday, I know that at this period of time and season of your lives, are very historical and special moments, full with great expectations, anxieties and anticipations, as both of you slowly, physically and mentally with much imagination fit yourselves into that rightful mood and mould for that arriving day of Bliss to come. I do hope as I daily remember both of you in my prayers that your nervousness and anxieties are under control as you both view yourselves in the Mirror of a new life of unity, oneness, passionate love, never ending happiness and lasting joy, sa both of you patiently await the arrival of that day to receive that miraculous moment of BLESSINGS, as both say "I do!" While the whole world, heaven and earth and all creations, cheer, salute and rejoice with thundering of rejoicing, as witnesses of this 'Royal of Royalties Honoured Unforgettable World Salute God Blessed Occasion,' not forgetting the main Host, God the Father, God the Son, God the Holy Spirit.

Prince Williams and Kate Middleton, my name is John Adolphus Hodge, a servant of the Most High God. I am a blood-bought, blood-washed child of God. I gave my heart to the Lord at the tender age of thirteen. Presently, I am fifty-six years old. I have two children, Lynelle (my daughter) and Tristan (my son), and one grandson, Landon. I grew up with a God-fearing mother who spent practically all her life ministering the Word of God throughout our little island of St. Kitts, Leeward Islands, West Indies. She had us her eight children as her only congregation on weekends as she ministered the Word of God; in the open-air, private homes, old-age homes, and private homes with sick or shut-in folks, in the hospitals, in the neighbourhood, to our school friends, and all with whom she came in contact throughout her life.

My beloved mother was blessed with eight children consisting of four boys and four girls. At very early ages of our lives, our loving mother introduced us to the Word of God. She did not stay home and send us to Church and Sunday school, but she happily took us. Mommy as we lovingly delighted in calling her, took us on endless marathon journeys on many occasions showing and teaching us as much as she can about God, His goodness, mercy, love, peace, grace and how to know, live and imitate Him as we follow him each day of our lives. Most importantly, mommy instilled within us memory verses and passages of the Bible scriptures for our daily spiritual warfare. Then finally at the age of seventy-seven years our loving mother closed her eyes singing, "My soul magnified the Lord, and my spirit praise His name. Even death could not hold Him captive, even in the grave, He is Lord!" When God's will, plans and purposes were all fulfilled He called her home to a place of rest. I can say confidently that my mother lives a well satisfied life, and was blessed with the privilege of seeing all eight of us her children, giving our lives to the Lord. Our loving mother was our mentor, mother, doctor, nurse, teacher, minister, guide and all that a true loving mother can be. I always referred to out loving mother as, 'An Angel of Love sent from heaven above'!

Prince William and Kate Middleton, it is with great honour and with most delightful pleasure for me to have received the privilege of this assigned duty to perform, of letting both of you know that the Lord God Almighty has approved, signed and stamped the Union, Unity and Oneness of your 'Marriage,' against all forces of negativity.

On the 14th January, 2011, at 4.45 am, in a vision/dream the Lord showed me both of you, seated in a quiet place on the grass in a park, happily searching the Bible, while Kate was eagerly reading, and you were quietly listening giving her your undivided attention as she read from the Word of God to you.

This dramatic scene truly blessed my heart, knowing it was God showing me the full approval of his plans, Purposes and Will for your life together as One-United-Union. So He wanted me to let you both know, 'your union together, it is real; all your doubts are settled, and this was done by God the Father, God the Son, God the Holy Spirit long before the world began. The Epistle of Titus 1:2 reads, "In hope of eternal life, which God that cannot lie promise before the world began." As I looked at Kate reading the Bible to you (Prince William), the Lord reminded me of Psalm 131. This is a picture of what she looked like as she humbly read from the Bible. The title of this Psalm is, "Humility before the Lord."

"LORD, my heart is not haughty, nor mine eyes lofty: neither do I exercise myself in great matters, or in things too high for me. Surely I have behaved and quieted myself, as a child that is weaned of his mother: my soul is even as a weaned child, Let Israel hope in the LORD from henceforth and forever."

I am also thinking of the words of a well-known song: It's Real!
But at last I tired of living such a life of fear and doubt,
For I wanted God to give me something I would know about,
So the truth would make me happy, and the light would clearly shine,
And the Spirit give assurance that I'm his and he is mine.

Chorus
But it's real, it's real, it's real,
O I know, I know, it's real,
Praise God, the doubts are settled,
For I know, I know it's real!

Prince William, Kate Middleton is not just a helpmeet given to you, as God refers to all wives, but she is God's precious Gift to you. Before the world began, God has chosen her and specially had her set-apart for you to wed; this is not luck or chance, but God's Will, Plan and Purpose for this time and season for both your lives. Kate Middleton, Prince William is not just God's special Gift to you, but he is forever-blessed, uniquely special, chosen and holy to the Lord. In the Gospel of Luke 2:23, God Himself said long before creation, "As it is written in the law of the Lord, Every male that openeth the womb shall be called holy to the Lord." Because of this statement from God, Kate, you, too, are richly blessed with the blessings that God has bestowed upon him. Further, because of that, both of you can say together, "We are blessed! We are blessed! We are blessed, all because of God's Will, Plan and Purpose for our lives, as He approved, stamped and signed our 'marriage,' long before any creation."

As we look one more step further, we can see the clear evidence of God's approval. We can see the Spirit of God at work, as the Honourable Prime Minister David Cameron announced that on the date of the wedding, Saturday 29th April, 2011, is now declared a public holiday, when the whole country come together as one, as we UNITE, as one rejoicing and celebrating with Prince William and our new Princess, Kate Middleton, on their 'WEDDING DAY,' as we and the rest of the world join together as we you union our share of blessings! This was seconded in motion and jointly agreed as a bond of Unity by the leader of the opposition Labour Party, the Honourable Ed Miliband and the entire house. This reminds me of the bond of UNITY; Unity is Love and Unity is God! In Psalm 117, we can see that the truth of the Lord endureth forever, "O Praise the Lord, all ye nations: praise him, all ye people. For his mercifulness kindness is great towards us: and the truth of the Lord endureth for ever. Praise ye the Lord." Then, in a song in Psalm 67, the Psalmist reminds us of the blessings and the benefits man receives when all the Nations unite together as one in rejoicing with thanksgiving and praise to the Lord for what He has done.

Psalm: 67, 'God be merciful upon us, and bless us; and cause his face to shine upon us; Selah. That thy way may be known upon earth, thy saving health among all nations. Let the people praise thee, O God; let all the people praise thee. O let the nations be glad and sing for joy: for thou shalt judge the people righteously, and govern the nations upon earth, Selah. Then shall the earth yield her increase; and God, even our own God shall bless us. God shall bless us; and all the ends of the earth shall fear him.'

Prince William and Kate Middleton, as I close this word of revelation from the Lord God Most High, I now pray and continue to pray, that your joy may be full and overflowing with the Divine Blessing of God on your appointed 'Royal Blessed Wedding Day,' as you both give God a standing-ovation of raised hands of Praise and Thanks to, God the Father, God the Son, God the Holy Spirit, for all what He has done, presently doing and all He promised to do for both of you and future family, throughout the unknown future. May the goodness, mercy, peace, protection, guide and love of the Lord Jesus Christ reign throughout your entire God blessed lives. I invite you to give God your hearts and allows him to be the builder of your lives. God loves both of you, and so do I! And I will never cease praying for both of you, the whole Royal family, the country and the rest of the world.

Finally I have already placed your names of the church prayer list where continued prayers are and will continue going up to God's throne of grace on your behalf. Also I am giving both you Prince William your tender, loving, pretty and passionate Princess Kate Middleton, an early and warm invitation to come and pay us a visit, and enjoy a time of sweet fellowship with us, as we worship and give thanks to the Lord God Almighty at this address. The PILGRIM CHURCH, Queens Walk, Meadows, Nottingham, NG2 2DF, and Telephone: 0115 986 5633 www.thepilgrimchurch.co.uk Email: thepilgrimchurch@yahoo.co.uk.

Yours sincerely

John A Hodge
Servant of the Most High God.

United States of America
USA God Has Chosen You!
Jer U. S. A.lem

A t some times in life, we know that we are a very important fig-
urative contributor to life, but still do not know the full magnitude of the powerful positive influence and impact we have in our
home, family, community, at work, to our country or nation and even
the world over. Until it is drawn to our attention, by someone, or
some supernatural God given voice.

Often we have heard of true stories of people, working with each
other in love and harmony, and for some reason spiritually have drawn
together and became good friends. Then finally affectionately attached,
and after years of razor blade friendship, one day surprisingly discovered not only they are friends, but bones of bone, and blood of blood,
miraculously fleshly family related.

In the Bible, in St. Luke: 24 vs 15—53. We have a picture of Jesus in
the company of His disciples, and others, after His resurrection walking
and talking with them and yet they all were unaware of whose company
in which they were in until Jesus finally identified and revealed Himself.

Today while on one of my usual weekly period of prayer and fasting,
God The Holy Spirit, gave me this 'Revelation' of which He commands
me to write to you, 'United States of America,' and for the whole world
to know and be aware of. I know people will be asking. How do you
know that this is what God really wants you to do? Answer. On Sunday,
18ᵗʰ January, 2009, I got full Conformation and Approval by God The

Holy Spirit, while attending church on that Sunday morning, during the delivering of the message, by His Servant. This Servant of God were unaware on that Sunday morning who this message were directly spoken to, but knew it was directed to one in that present congregation, and I knew immediately it was me. Because I were in the process of writing this same 'Revelation,' unknown to anyone, but listening for the Conformation and Approval which I received.

This 'Revelation' clearly showing a picture of true relationship of The United States of America and Israel. For many years now, The United States of America and Israel shares a special bond of true love and friendship which continues to grow and it is growing stronger and stronger every day. This intimate bond of love can be described as 'O Perfect Love.' It is 'Not Like,' a marriage made in heaven, but it 'IS' indeed a marriage that was made, Confirmed and Approved, by God the Father, God the Son, 'God the Holy Spirit, 'IN HEAVEN,' long before the world began. Within the marriage vow, we have the words of oath, 'for better for worst, for richer or poorer, till death do us part'!

This rich bond of love, in the past has caused vexations between USA and a number of its 'Allies' and even at present this same operations still continues. Many of her Allies are angry with Israel, just wagging their tails, but knows they cannot do anything touching Israel.

In the past The United States of America's 'Presidents,' even the last one President, George W. Bush (Son), who just left office, two weeks ago, and passed on the keys/baton to the new President, Barack H. Obama. This is what he said in his last statement in relation to Israel's and their conflict in Gaza. President George W. Bush, said, 'Israel' must defend herself'! This in itself finally summarized the true rich bond of forever growing Love between USA and Israel.

In the past all those elected Presidents, immediately after taking the oath of office of President of The Great United States of America, continued the role and relationship of 'Big Brother to Little Brother Israel,' whether Republican or Democrat, including the other three living Presidents. President; Jimmy L Carter, George H. W. Bush and William Bill. J. Clinton. All these Presidents immediately started supporting, looking after and always on the defence of Little Brother Israel. This continued bond of love relationship often causes many people of race, colour, language, creed, countries, and nations, either verbally or silently to raise this key question. What is the history of this bond of love affair between The Great United States of America and Israel?

Neither the United States of America, which included all the forty fourth (44) Presidents, all Republicans, Democrats and all its citizens. Also all Israelites and the rest of the world, knows the true history of this 'Undying-Love.'

Again this history of undying, rich, forever bond of love relationship started thousands of years long before the world began. This is God Himself words. This were drawn up in God's original plans, long before anything was created.

Kindly get your King James Version Bible and turn to the second to last book of the Old Testament, to Zachariah: 2 vs 1–2, and you will read these words. As Zachariah continues his duty and calling of God's Prophet, as God reveals Himself to him, showing and discussing with him the hidden and secrets things that is hidden from man. God them gave the Prophet Zachariah this 'Revelation' concerning the 'Brother relationship of Israel and The United States of America. This is what God said to him in verse one and two, reads, 'And he showed me Joshua the high priest standing before the angel of the LORD, and Satan standing at his right hand to resist him. And the LORD said unto Satan, the LORD rebuke thee, O Satan even the LORD that hath chosen Jerusalem (JerU.S.A.lem) rebuke thee; is not this a brand plucked out of the fire?

The LORD God, has chosen the United States of America (USA), long before the world began, as part of His drawn-up plan to performed two main duties on this earth. a) To be Big Brother to little Brother Israel. b) To be the Super Power of this world keeping 'World-Peace.'

God knew Israel would become a target for many a Nations, so He has 'CHOOSEN, the GREAT UNITED STATES OF AMERICA,' the World's main Super-Power, to be Israel's Big Brother, best earthly friend, supporter and defender, at all times forever.' If God chose you, you will always come through on top, because He is with you and when God is with anyone he or she cannot and will not fail.

For many years now, The United States of America and Israel has being walking hand in hand displaying a passionate love affair for each other, caused many a Nations and Allies to get angry and jealous, not knowing this is what God Himself has chosen and ordained long before the world began.

> Within this revelation that God gave to His Prophet Zachariah, the Lord said unto Satan, "I rebuke thee, O Satan even the Lord that hath chosen JerU.S.A.lem rebuke thee; is not this a brand plucked out of the fire?"

> If the LORD is speaking of JerU.S.A.lem, then He must be referring to the United States of America (USA), because the USA is the centre of JerU.S.A.lem in Israel. This means that the USA, was also a brand plucked out of the fire and out of Satan's hand.

> Since USA is the Heart of JerU.S.A.lem of Israel, which means it has a big and serious role to play in the entire life of Israel. What is the role and function of the heart? The heart is the central pump of the entire body (Israel). It supplies the whole body with blood.

The heart protects, supports, unites, gives signals, and makes us happy. It is a symbol of love; it preserves, gives warning, looks after us, and we depend on it for survival. The heart is God's power engine for life, it is friendship for life, for better or for worse, for richer or poorer, till death do us part.

America because God has chosen you to be the centre, heart-beat and defender of Israel, then He has equipped, empowered, sustained and will continue because He has chosen you. Therefore, you have "a job to do, a standard to uphold, and a duty to perform," looking after your little Brother Israel. I therefore remind you of this vow to God, "In God We Trust!"

USA the Heart of Israel

UNITED STATES OF AMERICA GOD HAS CHOSEN YOU AS BIG BROTHER TO LITTLE BROTHER ISRAEL!

JERUSALEM

USA God has Lovingly chosen you. Long before the world began, as Big Brother to help Little Brother Israel, Live a God promised victorious life!

USA God has Strategically chosen you, Long before the world began, as Big Brother to help little Brother Israel, discharged its legal military duties!

USA God has Carefully chosen you, Long before the world began, as Big Brother to help little Brother Israel, sweeten its dreadful and bitter cup!

USA God has Specially chosen you, Long before the world began, as Big Brother to help little Brother Israel, smooth its rough and rugged roads!

USA God has Peacefully chosen you, Long before the world began, as Big Brother to help little Brother Israel, face its anger and endless struggles!

USA God has Uniquely chosen you, Long before the world began, as Big Brother to help little Brother Israel, overcome its awful miseries!

USA God has Politely chosen you, Long before the world began, as Big Brother to help little Brother Israel, erase its nervous tensions!

USA God has Dynamically chosen you, Long before the world began, as Big Brother to help little Brother Israel, bravely meets its numberless enemies challenges!

USA God has Understandingly chosen you, Long before the world began, as Big Brother to help little Brother Israel, lightened its increasing heavy burdens!

USA God has Preciously chosen you, Long before the world began, as Big Brother to help little Brother Israel, protects its pinnacle preciousness of life!

USA God has Loyally chosen you, Long before the world began, as Big Brother to help little Brother Israel, calm its troubled and stormy seas!

USA God has Pre-Creatively and Powerfully chosen you, long before the world began, as Big Brother to help little Brother Israel, presently, possesses, its powerful, précised, position, positively!

GOD'S GIFT OF INHERITANCE TO ISRAEL.

We are serving a God who cannot lie, will not lie and one who kept His promises forever. He remains the same yesterday, today and forever and His words are true.

God has made endless promises to the children of Israel, and a vast number of those promises have been fulfilled and a few more is left to come to past. The Lord Jesus promise to return, and we can see the time of His promised return is drawing near. If we continues to read His Word, we will clearly see that Israel is a very important symbol, because it signifies the time 'CLOCK,' of Jesus returns, and the things that is happening and taking place surrounds it (Israel) clearly tells His coming is very near.

God has made endless promises to the children of Israel, and here are few. If you can kindly get your hand on a King James Version, Bible and go the Old Testament, and turn with me to the Book of Isaiah: 41 vs 8 -29, this is the revelation of God to His prophet concerning His defence of the children of Israel. It reads, But thou, Israel, art my servant, Jacob whom I have chosen, the seed of Abraham my friend.

[9] Thou whom I have taken from the ends of the earth, and called thee from the chief men thereof, and said unto thee, Thou art my servant; I have chosen thee, and not cast thee away.

[10] Fear thou not; for I am with thee: be not dismayed; for I am thy God: I will strengthen thee; yea, I will help thee; yea, I will uphold thee with the right hand of my righteousness.

¹¹ Behold, all they that were incensed against thee shall be ashamed and confounded: they shall be as nothing; and they that strive with thee shall perish.

¹² Thou shalt seek them, and shalt not find them, even them that contended with thee: they that war against thee shall be as nothing, and as a thing of nought.

¹³ For I the Lord thy God will hold thy right hand, saying unto thee, Fear not; I will help thee.

14 Fear not, thou worm Jacob, and ye men of Israel; I will help thee, saith the Lord, and thy redeemer, the Holy One of Israel.

¹⁵ Behold, I will make thee a new sharp threshing instrument having teeth: thou shalt thresh the mountains, and beat them small, and shalt make the hills as chaff.

¹⁶ Thou shalt fan them, and the wind shall carry them away, and the whirlwind shall scatter them: and thou shalt rejoice in the LORD, and shalt glory in the Holy One of Israel.

¹⁷ When the poor and needy seek water, and there is none, and their tongue faileth for thirst, I the Lord will hear them, I the God of Israel will not forsake them.

¹⁸ I will open rivers in high places, and fountains in the midst of the valleys: I will make the wilderness a pool of water, and the dry land springs of water.

¹⁹ I will plant in the wilderness the cedar, the shittah tree, and the myrtle, and the oil tree; I will set in the desert the fir tree, and the pine, and the box tree together:

²⁰ That they may see, and know, and consider, and understand together, that the hand of the Lord hath done this, and the Holy One of Israel hath created it.

²¹ Produce your cause, saith the Lord; bring forth your strong reasons, saith the King of Jacob.

²² Let them bring them forth, and shew us what shall happen: let them shew the former things, what they be, that we may consider them, and know the latter end of them; or declare us things for to come.

²³ Shew the things that are to come hereafter, that we may know that ye are gods: yea, do good, or do evil, that we may be dismayed, and behold it together.

²⁴ Behold, ye are of nothing, and your work of nought: an abomination is he that chooseth you.

²⁵ I have raised up one from the north, and he shall come: from the rising of the sun shall he call upon my name: and he shall come upon princes as upon morter, and as the potter treadeth clay.

²⁶ Who hath declared from the beginning, that we may know? and beforetime, that we may say, He is righteous? yea, there is none that sheweth, yea, there is none that declareth, yea, there is none that heareth your words.

²⁷ The first shall say to Zion, Behold, behold them: and I will give to Jerusalem one that bringeth good tidings.

²⁸ For I beheld, and there was no man; even among them, and there was no counsellor, that, when I asked of them, could answer a word.

²⁹ Behold, they are all vanity; their works are nothing: their molten images are wind and confusion.

God is here reminding Israel and the entire world, that He is not slack concerning none of His promises to Israel and all mankind. Israel is the time clock, telling the time of His coming and He is saying, although Israel has an earthly 'Big Brother,' the United States of America, as her defence. He is saying, wherever USA fails, He is there prepared, watching, looking and ready to pick-up the slack defending Israel. God' Word is true and He never fails.

God is all Powerful, and He has all Power both in heaven and here on earth. And He has the Power to give to who so ever He chooses.

America God has chosen you and has given you this awesome Power, and makes you a Great and Mighty Awesome Powerful Nation. And no one can change the Power of God's; will, plans and purposes for you, but 'You America'! Not even Satan has such power to rearrange or change it.

America, God has chosen you long before the world began, just as He has chosen the Prophet Jeremiah, long before creation began, because He is God, Omnipotent, Omniscience and Omnipresence, there is not like Him past, present or future!

America, many of your fore-fathers, leaders and Presidents, who has gone on before, even those remaining four former Presents who is still alive, all Americans, the rest of the world and even your present President Barack H Obama, continue to wonder. What makes this

Country of USA so Great, Mighty and Powerful? The answer is 'But God! But God! But God's Hand of Choice, Will, Plan and Purpose'!

Revelation!

**The Danger of Changing God's Plans,
God's Gifts of Inheritance to Israel.**

Who has given you the Power, to Altar God's Plans?

He is going to Touch you!

Who has given you the Authority, to Rearrange God's Plans?

He is going to get Angry with you!

Who has given the Right, to Stop God's Plans?

He is going to Mobilize your movement!

Who has given you the Approval, to Discontinue God's Plans?

He is going to chastise you in His own time!

Who has given you the Idea, to Interfere with God's Plans?

He is going to Arrest you in His Prison!

Who has given you the Strength, to Break God's Plans?

He is going to totally destroy you!

Who has given you the Purpose, to Trouble God's Plans?

He is going to slue you, like Og the king of Basham!

God's Plans, Will and Purpose's must be fulfilled!

Take your hands off God's Plans!

Land is a precious and none perishable commodity, which has the potential to always appreciate. This is a commodity that brings lots of joy, and also lots of heartaches, enemies, sadness, conflicts, endless troubles and at times sad to say even death. This commodity when it is not handled properly, it has a way of forming a sad and bitter generational chain. This can be found among families and families, friends and friends, neighbours and neighbours, countries and also it can escalate to endless conflicts and even wars among nations.

Land is bought and sold for an agreed price between parties involved. Some people in the past, at present and I believe in the future, fell, falling and will continues to fall prey to the covetousness of it.

This is one of the oldest and major conflicts, which are robbing the peace of endless people in this world in which we are living in right now, especially when it comes to 'FAMILY INHERITANCE TO SHARE,' it brings nothing less than endless 'WARS AMONG FAMILIES.'

I hope you are not too tired turning to your Bible with me. If not kindly turn to the New Testament, (King James Version), to St. Luke: 12 vs 13 — 15. Here we have a glimpse of Jesus addressing and dealing with a case of family inheritance, which escalated into unbearable pain of 'Covetousness.'

Jesus while He was here on earth, during His earthly Ministry, people by the multitudes followed him for miles, from village to village, seeing the miracles which He did and hearing words of wisdom as He continues His earthly Ministry. Also during His Ministry, Jesus used endless parables that people can understand clearly what He was speaking about.

In the midst of one of His Ministry addressing the usual multitude of people, a shoe was not thrown at Him, which caused Him to duck, bob and weaves . . . like the former president George W Bush. No! But a man in the company of the multitude cried out in pain of an unbearable, family inheritance unsolved problem.

This man interrupted Jesus (The Master), as He was Ministering to the multitude of people, because he was angry with his brother, who refused him his full portion of an inheritance which he expected a full satisfying share, of which he was denied . . . This 'Sin of Covetousness,' takes place still among many a so-called families today!

So this man interrupted Jesus and shouted, 'Master, speak to my brother, that he divide the inheritance with me'!

Jesus, answered, "Man who make me a judge or a divider over you?" Then Jesus immediately turned to the multitude of people and said, "Take heed and beware of covetousness, for a man's life consisteth not in the abundant of things which he possesseth!"

For many years now we are hearing about Land for Peace in Israel. People are possessors of Land by various means. Some people own Lands by purchasing it, others own theirs by inheritance, while some own there's by stealing etc.

Kindly turn to Psalms 136:1–26 in the Old Testament of the Bible (KJV). Here we have a clear picture of the Power of God drawn and dramatized for all to see the displaying of the goodness and mercy of God to the Children of Israel, and how they got possession of their Land.

Psalm 136
[1] O give thanks unto the LORD; for he is good: for his mercy endureth for ever.
[2] O give thanks unto the God of gods: for his mercy endureth for ever.
[3] O give thanks to the Lord of lords: for his mercy endureth for ever.
[4] To him who alone doeth great wonders: for his mercy endureth for ever.
[5] To him that by wisdom made the heavens: for his mercy endureth for ever.
[6] To him that stretched out the earth above the waters: for his mercy endureth for ever.

[7] To him that made great lights: for his mercy endureth for ever:
[8] The sun to rule by day: for his mercy endureth for ever:
[9] The moon and stars to rule by night: for his mercy endureth for ever.
[10] To him that smote Egypt in their firstborn: for his mercy endureth for ever:
[11] And brought out Israel from among them: for his mercy endureth for ever:
[12] With a strong hand, and with a stretched out arm: for his mercy endureth for ever.
[13] To him which divided the Red sea into parts: for his mercy endureth for ever:
[14] And made Israel to pass through the midst of it: for his mercy endureth for ever:
[15] But overthrew Pharaoh and his host in the Red sea: for his mercy endureth for ever.
[16] To him which led his people through the wilderness: for his mercy endureth for ever.
[17] To him which smote great kings: for his mercy endureth for ever:
[18] And slew famous kings: for his mercy endureth for ever:
[19] Sihon king of the Amorites: for his mercy endureth for ever:
[20] And Og the king of Bashan: for his mercy endureth for ever:
[21] And gave their land for an heritage: for his mercy endureth for ever:
[22] Even an heritage unto Israel his servant: for his mercy endureth for ever.
[23] Who remembered us in our low estate: for his mercy endureth for ever:
[24] And hath redeemed us from our enemies: for his mercy endureth for ever.
[25] Who giveth food to all flesh: for his mercy endureth for ever.
[26] O give thanks unto the God of heaven: for his mercy endureth for ever.

Israel got their Land, by the Divine Power of the working of God Himself. The Children of Israel did not just go and settled, O, No! Neither did they just stopped and pull up their hand brake! It was not like that, 'ISRAEL GOT THEIR LAND by DIVINE INHERITANCE.' Not from the 'Inheritance,' of a King of another country. No Sir! Israel got their Land by God given 'Inheritance' to them.

Israel is the only country in the world where Land is not on sale. According to the Israel's Basic Law, state Lands cannot be sold, but it is usually least to individuals or institutions for a period of forty nine or ninety eight years (49 or 98 years). God's 'Inheritance,' cannot be sold, will not be sold, and exchanged, given away or otherwise! God's Divine Inheritance to Israel, His plans, and His works stands forever and ever Amen'!

TO PRESIDENT BARACK H OBAMA.

M r. President, this is short note of Congratulation of having entered into the season which God Himself has chosen for you to reign as President of the Most Powerful Mighty Nation, on earth. The United States of America, as one of His chosen Nation. And this appointed time of your reign, were Authorized and Approved by the 'Sweet will of God,' long before the world began! I must therefore bring to your awareness of all the former Presidents, who served, as President of the United States of America, that their elect as President, also were God's hand of choice, for that time, era and seasons of their service and reign.

President Barack H Obama, I am going to introduce to you four verses of Scriptures, of which I would like you and your family to spend a little time to memorize them and 'Say them,' (Speak them), each day in your own private time and meditate on them. And in doing so you and your family will be planting and sowing seeds of God's true wisdom into your lives, which will grow stronger and stronger every day, then when this is done, they will germinate, prosper and bring forth an abundant of generational harvest of fruits, consisting of life and light. And this end product too will continue to bear untold fruits, such as physical, spiritual, financial, moral, mental, God's true continued wisdom, knowledge and understanding. And all that you're 'Heart's Desires,' as you live obedient to His Holy Word.

Mr. President, the simple reason why I chose to say , 'Speak them,' and this is specific, because God Himself showed us by demonstrations, the Powerful results we receives when we actually 'Speak the word,' and not just the thought of it.

Mr. President, kindly spare me a brief moment of your tight schedule and turn with me to the Book of Proverbs in the Old Testament (KJV). Proverbs 18:21 reads, "Death and life are in the power of the tongue: and they that love it shall eat the fruit thereof." God Himself demonstrated to us, when he said, in Genesis 1:3, "And God said, let there be light: and there was light." God has spoken with the Power of His tongue and it was done.

Mr. President, God has given us the power of choice as we, 'Chooses,' to use our tongue. What we say with our own tongue is what we get in return when we speak the Word! Speaking the Word, is as simple as this example. If you, Mr. President, take a lawn tennis ball from the World Champion Serena Williams, and throws it against a wall, the results is simple, it will come back to you as it rebounds from off the wall, if you are standing directly in front the wall. Now, Sir, if you change and chose to use a gulf ball, then with all of you might, throws it, standing twenty feet away directly in front of the wall, then naturally you are asking for serious trouble. Because according to the force of nature, it will return with both speed and force and the end results can be catastrophic. This simply indicates, if we speaks bad or good things, they will comes back to us and followers us all the days of our life. So when these verses of scriptures is spoken into our lives each day, they results is blessings of divine-favour, hedges of protections, goodness, mercy, love, peace, and the grace of God following us all the days of our lives.

Sir, these are the verses of Scripture in 1 Chronicles 4:10, "And Jabez called upon the God of Israel saying, Oh that thou wouldest bless me indeed, and enlarged my coast, and that thine hand might be with me, and that thou wouldest keep me from evil, that it may not grieve me! And God grant him that which he requested."

Isaiah 50:4 reads, "The Lord God hath given me the tongue of the learned, that I should know how to speak a word in season to him that is weary: he wakeneth morning by morning, he wakeneth mine ear to hear as the learned."

Isaiah 54:17 reads, "No weapon that is formed against me shall prosper; and every tongue that shall rise against thee in judgment thou shalt condemn. This is the heritage of the servant of the servant of the Lord, and their righteousness is of me, saith the Lord."

Isaiah 55:11 reads, "So shall my word be that goeth forth out of my mouth: It shall not return unto me void, but it shall accomplished that which I pleased, and prosper in the things where to I sent it."

Sir, this is a bonus scripture verse. Titus 1:2 reads, "In Hope of eternal life, which God that cannot lie, promised before the world began."

Mr. President, please do not get weary, it was hard for me to eliminate this verse: "For I the Lord thy God will hold thy right hand, saying unto thee fear not; I will help thee" (Isa. 41:13).

Mr. President, Barack H Obama, God has allowed the late Civil Right Leader, Dr. Martin Luther King Jr; a glimpse into the future, where he has seen in his vision, you, Mr. Barack H Obama, then he verbally spoke the word, and by the power of his tongue it has come to pass/past. Again we have seen the evidence and results of speaking the word with the power of the tongue, life and light appeared.

Mr. President, the late Dr. Martin Luther King Jr; was blessed with the Gift of the Spirit, and at this time of this 'Revelation,' he was operating in 'the Gifts of Revelations,' this Gifts consists of three gifts; The Gift of the Word of Wisdom, the Gift of the Word of Knowledge and the Gift of Discerning of Spirits.' At this time Dr. King, were operating in the Gift of the Word of Wisdom, this Gift speaks of the present and the future. Like Moses, he was that Moses who saw the Promise-Land but was unable to enter. Then because he was not chosen to lead the people into the Promise-Land. But Joshua, then obviously because you were chosen then you Mr. President Barack H Obama, is indeed the chosen Joshua for this; time, era and season to lead the people, not only to be the President of the Great United States of America, but also to the rest of the world, who is looking to you for help, leadership and directions.

Mr. President, God has chosen you long before the world began, because of who you are. God has created you and blessed you with all the Skills, Technology and Leadership role that the people will welcome with open hearts and arms. You were chosen because you were created, 'Multi'; colour, nationality, creed, language, culture and understanding, also because you are young, vibrant and strong.

Then Mr. President, it is time for forgiveness, healing, unity, oneness, togetherness, love, peace, and fellowship. This is why God has chosen you for this period of time, era, and season, surrounding you with four living former Presidents: President George W. Bush, William Bill J. Clinton, George H.W. Bush and Jimmy L. Carter. We have able Democrats, vibrant Republicans, and visionary Independents, whom you can call upon for help and direction if needed. Pick up your phone and get their assistance, because now they understand that they, too, were chosen by God for that time and season of their service, leadership, and reign. The Great United States of America was chosen long before the world began. Therefore, they will not deny you assistance, knowing it's not for you but for the benefit of "The Greatest and Mighty Powerful Nation on earth," the United States of America, which they once ruled and served.

Finally, God is Love and love is God. Because He loves you, the Great United States of America and the rest of the world, this is a reminder that Divine Retribution correction, and rebuke is also part of God's plans and ways of punishing and arresting us when we tends to go astray from the path He has laid out for us. God corrects those whom He loves, and His Love is Unconditional.

Mr. President, God loves you and family, I love you and family and the rest of the world loves you and family. Now, God wants you to love 'ALL MEN,' everywhere. Again speaking the word is very powerful and important. Speaking it for the whole-world to hear, tell the; blacks, white, Asians, Chinese, Cubans, Muslins and all other nations, faiths and religions of your love for them.

Mr. President, I am praying for you, and I know that the multitudes and millions of people too are also praying for you and we will continue our prayers, for you and family, The Great United States of America and the rest of the world. You are not alone! God bless you! Continue to give God thanks! He is Worthy! 'In God We Trust'!

The "Seas" Turned Jet Black.

In this dream, God the Holy Spirit showed me the SEAS turning JET BLACK three or four months before Libya's leader died.

People Jesus is coming and all that we are experiencing are signs leading up to His second return to this earth, which is the Rapturing or taking away or snatching away of His church, which means those who opened their hearts and let Him in, or those who are 'Saved' by His grace, blood-bought, blood-washed children of God! Jesus loves us and are warning us (Mankind), saying, prepare yourself because I am coming sooner that you can ever imagine. I know this saying sounds like an old long-time slogan, a repetitious or stick record . . . this is giving all men ample time, having no excuse whatsoever. God is using me (His Servant), at this present; moment, era, time and season, to remind you that this is no joke, no slogan, no bed-time-story and no fairy-tale but all truth! People remember those people in Noah's days? Those same people were people like us today, who listened to the preaching of His Servant Noah, who preached for 120 years, yet those people gave him a deaf ear and refused to believe the message of the truth, which were their final warning. They believed when it were too late! Noah's; preaching, warning, pleading, begging, encouraging and pursuing all ended!

People, do you know what Noah were preaching about? Noah were preaching on this same topic, that the whole-world is presently dealing with today, God the Holy Spirit, called me, manifested Himself to me gave me all these 'Revelations' to share with you, to tell you and to preach to you about this same climate change which is God's final warning to mankind! In the days of Noah, there was no rain falling form the sky as we know it today. Their water came up from the ground, which was call a mist. So when Noah preached about the falling of rain from the heavens, they all looked at him and classified him as a crazy man. Today, we would have done the same thing. In Noah's days, there was no past example for them to learn from, but today, we have every reason to be different, because but we have Noah and those people as our example. If we fail to believe the Message and the Messenger God sends with His final warning, we have no one to blame but our own selves. Matthew 24:34–39 reads:

[34] Verily I say unto you, This generation shall not pass, till all these things be fulfilled.

[35] Heaven and earth shall pass away, but my words shall not pass away.

[36] But of that day and hour knoweth no man, no, not the angels of heaven, but my Father only.

[37] But as the days of Noah were, so shall also the coming of the Son of man be.

[38] For as in the days that were before the flood they were eating and drinking, marrying and giving in marriage, until the day that Noah entered into the ark,

[39] And knew not until the flood came, and took them all away; so shall also the coming of the Son of man be.

God finally closed or shut the 'Door of the Ark' because mankind rejected His loving kindness and tender mercy towards them! Today we are most privilege to have the presence of God's love, the gift of His Son, the Lord Jesus, still offering us of His loving-kindness and tender-mercy! Are we going to do like these people, bluntly rejects His open Door offers of Eternal life to us? If we rejects entering God's open Door, it will one day be shut on us! Then the rain began to fall . . . they believed at that moment but then it was too late! Those people allowed Satan to deceive themselves, saying, you still have time you can do it later! Folks kindly avoid the same mistake, there's no second chance! This is not just climate change, no, this is getting you to understand and believe His coming is true and very near!

In the fourth Book of the Gospel, John the Baptist were chosen by God the Father to be the four-runner of Jesus Christ, bearing the message to the people, saying 'Repent' of your sinfulness!

In the last Book of the Bible, in the Book of Revelations, God the Father has chosen another John, John the Revelatory, bearing the Revelation of Jesus Christ, the 'Rapture,' the message of Hope, for all mankind who choose to believe the message and the messenger. Both John's bearing that same message, 'Repent,' of your sinfulness and be prepared Jesus is coming soon!

God the Holy Spirit has chosen another John (yours truly), God the Father, have a special 'Love' for the 'John's.' John the Baptist was the Son of Elizabeth, who was the cousin of Mary the mother of Jesus. Both John the Baptist and Jesus are cousins and were born in the same year just months apart of each other. John the Baptist was the four-runner of Jesus and also baptised Jesus in the river Jordon.

In this dream, God the Holy Spirit, called me and entrusted me with this another one of His many revelations. The SEAS World-Wide turning JET BLACK, all connected to climate change. In this dream, God the Holy Spirit took me to the Island of my birth, beautiful St. Kitts, Leeward Islands, West Indies, in the Capital which is Basseterre, on the Bay Road of the Bayfront, where I stood viewing the endless miles of the sea flowing out as far as my eyes could behold. This viewing of the sea, which all of my growing-up years were all 'Blue-Wide-Oceans of Seas,' now standing in front of me all turning JET BLACK! This sight leaves me in wonderland, like that character, Alice in that children story, 'Alice in Wonderland'! I stood there spell-bound, viewing this extraordinary scene feeling and fighting for words which never appears, leaved me totally captivatedly speechless. What a sight it was for me to behold. It was indeed the dramatic scene that instantly brought home the true message to everyone: climate change is here, and it is serious and real.

Basseterre Bay Road, were jam packed with people from all walks of life and from every nuke and cranny living and holidaying on the Island. It was less than standing room only, for a fitting of even a needle space. Everyone stood with wide open eyes viewing with their mouths wide-open, most people so startled not knowing what to say. How can one find the right words describing this amazing miracle change of the Vast-Wide-Oceans-of-Blue-Seas, turning instantly JET BLACK?

During this frightening scene people draws close to the shores of the sea, and everyone doing their own science checks, trying to figure out for themselves the real cause of such miraculous change. When I first saw the changing of the water looking jet black, I started sniffing the atmosphere, trying to figure out what kind of gas is involved in the colouring of the Wide-Oceans-of-Seas. I was sniffing for the scent of gas, tar, and oils, all of which I received no evidence of whatsoever. But looking off in a long distant on the surface of the sea, it resembled a bright shiny glassy looks like a flat mirror in the disappearing distant. Cautiously I drew closer on the sand without shoe feeling the texture of the water with my feet, then with my hands feeling to see if the water is feeling as it usually do or if it is a bit thicker. The water felt the same as the usual I knew it to be. The only thing that seems to change to me was the colour of the water turning from 'BLUE TO JET BLACK'! Everyone were amazingly involved doing their own testing and feeling, making their own adventurous discoveries. This was the end of an era, time, season and age of the ever once colour of the world-wide-blue oceans-of-sea. Now everyone understand a little of what climate change, is all about and the great effects and forever changes it has caused on the whole out look of all living organism and creatures—both great and small.

I knew without the shadow of a doubt that everyone (the whole world) is shaking in their boots and is aware that this is indeed a major sign pointing toward the end of time, the soon return of Jesus to this world. What is the true condition of man's heart in turning from his unrighteous ways and style of living? People this is one of the signs that speaks loud and clear to mankind, saying. Stop, look and listen! It is time to make that once and for all eternal decision, either eternal life enjoying the place Jesus gone to prepare for all who trust Him or eternal damnation and punishment with Satan and his fallen angels in hell. People this is not causing you fear, no. It is telling you the truth and the whole truth!

Looking at the colour of the sea turning JET BLACK, I can instantly glimpse the clear sign of death and destruction for more than one third of the earth's populations. Creatures both great and small will be destroyed: mankind, animals, birds, plants, 90% percent of fish, mammals, and life in the sea! It is the shortening of the lifespan of all life on the entire earth. This will yield the most serious and catastrophic results, known as climate change. Earth's scientists are doing their best, but without the involvement of God in all we do, it results in null and void. The Psalmist reminds us of this most important matter.

Psalm 127:1 reads, "Except the Lord build the house they labour in vail that build it." If we are building, naturally we are going to seek for the best ever expert help and advice, helping us to achieved the best success in whatever our; ideas, goals, dreams and visions are, resulting in a strong foundation and great long-last results. Then if we fails to give God and invitation asking for His advice and help, then our projects or goals will results in great lacks, null, void and waste of energy and time. Without His helps, advice and inputs we will be always, guessing, wondering and fearing the true results. Are we at a point where our best learned and brilliant scientists has reach a limited point and are afraid to admit . . . Only God can help us now? Pride has played a most destructive role in many a people life simply because of fear and self-pride. The Bible clearly said, 'Pride' goeth before destructions, God loves honesty, true heart wrenching confessions and when we acknowledges our point of limitations humbling ourselves God will happily rewards us with His 'True wisdom' knowledge and understanding where every He sees fit and if there's a need.

People God is the Creator of everything, including the earth, dry land, the sea, and all living creatures on earth, in the air, and in the seas. He also said there is a "time and a season" for everything. In the field of sports, there is an Umpire or a Referee directing, giving orders, and controlling every aspects of whatever sport is in question. In the days of Noah, God looked down from His windows and seen the bad behaviour of mankind which makes Him unhappy. Lovingly He sends messages and warnings, saying, adjust and control your behaviour. The people in Noah's day stubbornly refused to listen and obey—both the messages and the messenger. God blew His whistle, trying to get their attention and bring order when things got out of hand, yet the people still refused to take orders. Then, He send His faithful, patience, and obedient servant, Noah with the final warning. He said, "Time out. Everything has changed; it is time for climate change! Noah preached for one hundred and twenty years until God was happy. The stubborn people refused to turn and they all perished in the flood. Presently, here on Earth, we are behaving like those people in Noah's day. God is angry with us because He send us numerous messages and warnings, yet we are behaving the same as the people in Noah's time. This is the reason God blew His whistle on us saying, "time out." With all these final warnings, these Messages of warning and practical things (climate change) for us to see, we know He is serious and His coming is very near!

God's knows just what is best for us and He created all the thing we are in need of in abundantly supply. In His work of creation He created the seas for us. Genesis 1:20–22 reads, "And God said, Let the waters bring forth abundantly the moving creatures that hath life, and fowl that may fly above the earth in the open firmament of heaven. And God created great whales, and every living creature that moveth, which the waters brought forth abundantly, after their kind, and every winged fowl after his kind: and God saw that it was good. And God blessed them, saying, Be fruitful, and multiply, and fill the waters in the seas, and let fowl multiply in the earth."

People, God is now saying to us, "time out" during this climate change crisis. He is reducing not only life in the sea, but in general. I am referring to the "food chain" of man, which will be minimized. Since the sea is now jet black, God's sunlight will not be able to penetrate the blackness of the water, which provides oxygen for all the living creatures, as well as the means for reproduction and sustenance. We need the sea for the continuation of mankind. It all depends on this food chain. People, I beg you, please do not wait for all these things to take place; give you heart and life to God right now before anything else takes place! Let me just give you a small fraction or pointers what to expect when the SEAS TURN JET BLACK.

Without God's sunlight, photosynthesis would not be able to take place. What is photosynthesis? Photosynthesis is a process which all green plants go through, they gets the energy from God's sunlight and used it to transport and transform water, carbon dioxide and other useful minerals into oxygen and organic compounds. This form of reaction shows us the important and effectiveness of God's sunlight in the continuations and sustenance of life and food chain for; mankind, animals and plants. This same photosynthesis manufactured for us most of the oxygen we needs helping us to breathe. Then we let out or exhale the carbon dioxide and the plants manufacture it for their own use. Plants are very important, it is a source of food, both to us as human being and the animals that we also eat. Therefore, because the sunlight cannot penetrate the Jet Black Sea, 90% of fish, mammals, plants, and all other living organism will surely die.

Then, after the death of all these people, the whole world will be at a health risk, causing a world-wide epidemic. The atmosphere will be highly polluted with the stench of death for years, causing the death of the remaining life in the seas, mankind within close surroundings, and even animals and plants on land. One more question: who can move and burry all these dead fishes and mammals from the Seas? Where will you burry them? It is impossible! This is only the start of the calamity of climate change, which is to come. This experience alone can be so strong it can cause man from cease living, putting a total end to man. This experience exceeds the dropping of an atomic bomb anywhere on earth because everybody feels it and suffers from its effects!

All sea traffic will be permanently stopped and ceased, such as living and travelling. Imports and exports by sea will be impossible, because the whole surface of the world will be impassable and blocked up by the millions of dead mammals and fishes. Just imagines what this will look like. Millions of people will be trapped at sea in large tourist cruise ships, oil tankers, warships, submarines, etc. This will be paralyzing the whole operations of mankind, both by air and at sea. Another large percentage of the remaining population will die due to the lack of transportation and shortage of gas, oil, and food for survival. Climate change is a reminder that Jesus is coming; get ready and be prepared.

If the sea is jet black, it would not be able to functions and actively carry out its role as usual and this will be detrimental in every areas of life in general. In the case of the sunlight. The sea adsorbs a lot of the light from the sun and a number of functions is carried out by this action. If the sea is jet black and cannot absorbs all that sunlight.

What will happen them to that volume of heat and energy from the sun? Would that extra volume of heat and energy bring destruction to earth and its surroundings, Mr. Scientist? Would the volume of heat and energy destroy man and his surroundings, including animals, plants, and other materials which can be melted by fervent heat? Would it cause a destructive heat wave destroying transformers and the like? Naturally, when the sea absorbs this volume of heat and energy from the sun, it helps to cool the earth in general! People, get ready, because Jesus is coming very soon!

The sea is very important in the life of man, animals, plants, and all living organism. The Sea plays a vital role in almost everything on earth, in the atmosphere, in the first and second heaven, and beyond. For example:

a) The reflection of the light from the sea plays a vital role in the bright reflection of light on earth, and earth's reflections to outer space.

b) It plays a great role in the reflection of the moon, stars, and all surrounding planets known to man.

c) It contributes to the clouds and their activities.

d) It is important in the contrasting colours of the rainbow, which remind us of God's promise to mankind.

e) It has a lot to do with reflections of colours we see and can identify.

f) It is very important in the greenhouse operation systems.

g) The volume of energy the sea absorbs lessens the melting of the ice in Greenland, the North Pole, and Antarctica. This eliminates endless tsunamis that cause destruction.

h) It also helps to cool the atmosphere around volcanoes throughout the entire world, keeping them less active.

EXCEPT The LORD Build The House, They Labour In Vain That Build It:

EXCEPT the LORD build the house,
They Labour in vain that build it:

Give God an invitation as your builder,

See Him at work in all areas of your life,
And experience Positive, Powerful, and Precious Victories.

EXCEPT the LORD build your Life,
Your parents worked in vail that build it.
EXCEPT the LORD build your Home,
Your contractor worked in vain that build it.
EXCEPT the LORD build your Sporting-Careers; tennis, cricket,
football and gulf etc.
Your Coach worked in vain that build it.
EXCEPT the LORD build you're Courtship,
The Love-birds worked in vain that build it.
EXCEPT the LORD build your Marriage,
Your Counsellors worked in vain that build it.
EXCEPT the LORD build you're Business,
The partners worked in vain that build it.
EXCEPT the LORD build you're Field of Education,
You're Teachers and Professor worked in vain that build it.
EXCEPT the LORD build the Government,
The Politician worked in vain that build it.
EXCEPT the LORD build the House of Congress,
The Committee and parties worked in vain that build it.
EXCEPT the LORD build the House of Lords, Commons and
Parliament,
The involving parties and committees worked in vain that build it.
EXCEPT the LORD build the Church,
EXCEPT the LORD build your Ideas, Dreams, and Visions,
EXCEPT the LORD build your Goals,
EXCEPT the LORD build you're Fortune,
Peter, David, Elizabeth, Fidel, Lynelle, Jesse, Marcella, Sarah, Denzil
and Hillary,
They all Labour in vain that build it.
Give the LORD an 'INVITATION,' and let Him do the building!

Author John A. Hodge.

HOT CLIMATIC COUNTRIES AND THE CARIBBEAN WILL EXPERIENCE BLIZZARDS OF SNOW STORMS.

C limate change has been experienced by all living organism on earth, creatures both great and small. Climate change is so serious; it is the greatest ever challenge to mankind. It has tested the best brains that earth has ever produced, resulting in our failure. With both hands raised to the heavens, we must surrender. Today, mankind needs to understand there is only one Creator and that is the Trinity/ God Head: God the Father, God the Son, and God the Holy Spirit. He is the only Creator of everything, both in the heavens and on the earth. God created mankind and He knows just what's best for us in our bodies, souls, and minds. When we go astray from God and His plans for us, we stumble, lose our way, and fall. We fall because we fail to follow the pathway, road, and guidance He provides for us. Mankind sets himself up as a "little god" and expects to be wor-shipped! In spite of our behaviour, God still loves us unconditionally, even if we fail to love Him, disobediently choosing the wrong way.

People God 'Created' us and His love for us is a dying-love, He loves us unto death, this is the reason He gave us His only begotten Son (Jesus) who gave His life for us, who laid down His life, died on the cross in our room paying the price for our sins, because we were unable and unworthy to pay the price for our sins. This is the reason He sends messengers warning us (the world populations), when danger is ahead, that we can prepare ourselves for the danger ahead. God has called, chosen, prepared, revealed Himself to me and send me with this message of warning to you, before the coming danger and judgment ahead.

God do not, would not and cannot reveals Himself to anyone who is not intimate with Him, flowering in His footsteps and fails to meet His required standards of His righteous expectations. Therefore, when God choose you to be His; voice, hands and feet, messenger and prophet to carry His word and message to the people of this entire world, He is satisfied because you meets His expected requirement and He is happy to use you by revealing Himself to you.

Climate change is nothing to taken lightly or slightly, but a change everyone needs to take very serious because we are facing and entering a life of uncertainty or unknown expectations. Climate change are full of surprises that at any times can change the whole course of life's journey, not only for mankind but can be extended to almost every living organism living in such environment. And this dramatic change from hot to cold can be one of those Climate change that will have a life-time change, which all will be experiencing and will be most financially costly for everyone. Throughout life journey there are many changing scenes altering man's total general plans!

In this dream, God the Holy Spirit showed me where the Hot Climatic Countries, Nations and Islands, will be experiencing 'Blizzards of Snow Storms,' due to climate change. How soon and for how long? I do not know yet! Would it be a one off or seasonal? I cannot say at this moment!

God the Holy Spirit, in a dream, took me to my Island of birth: The Land of Beauty, Beautiful St. Kitts, Leeward Island, and West Indies. There, in the capital (Basseterre), I experienced the first ever blizzard in the Caribbean. I do not remember what time of the year it was but everything resembled a typical "white Christmas." The streets were deserted, I started wondering if I am the only living one on the Island. I believed everyone were in a state of shock, fright and not far from having panic-attacks, mentally paralyzed, with their thoughts floating in space, not knowing what to do and where to start from. The place was totally paralyzed. I believed my people had a first-hand experienced of what it is like, not only singing, but practically experiencing their first ever "Silent Night."

I received most of these Revelations here in Great Britain and I kept sharing them with people in the church I attended, different Pastors, Ministers in UK, USA, and the Caribbean, different heads of governments and responsible heads etc. I remember saying to Caribbean people living in Great Britain, to stop disposing of their winter clothing, save them and send them home because our people will soon have great need of them. This climate change, thus far has caused a lot of changes and this is not even the tip of the ice-burg yet. People are you mentally feeling the effects of this new experience before it actually takes place? This is the first step of survival.

In the Caribbean a lot of these Islands are too small to be having one Political Party, ruling for five years, it is a waste of ideas, dreams, talents, and visions. Some Politicians never get the opportunity to use their 'Visions' for the benefit of the Island and people. Therefore, all these Political Parties need to 'Unite' as one for the benefit of everyone. Avoiding the 'Five Foolish Virgin Syndrome.' This may sound like a joke but presently there is a great need for this union. During the real heat of climate change there will be a need for all hands on deck! One Political Party cannot handle these kind of escalating pressure and headaches! Unity is Oneness, Unity is Strength, Unity is Love, Unity is Power and Unity is God! The Psalmist said, "Except the Lord, build the house, they labour in vain that build it." I did not say the Labour Party! Give God an invitation and let Him guide, direct and help in all your building process.

When this dream, were revealed to me concerning the climate change and the results of 'Blizzards of Snow,' falling in hot climatic countries and Islands, that same year, I can remembered vividly writing to a number of heads of government and people I know shows interest in Climate change and had them informed with the latest revelation. Involved were the present Prime Minister of U.K, David Cameron, the President of USA, and gave a little of my own suggestions. I reminded them about the seriousness and the struggles Caribbean Islands will be experiencing and the kind of help we will be greatly in needs of, both during the Rising Seas causing tsunamis and the falling of snow in the hot climate countries and islands.

I explained to them that since these experiences will be new to us, we will be like blind bats flying around not knowing where to go and what to do because of new system. I suggested that in the case of 'Snow falling,' we are going to be greatly in need of equipment and operators with Salt to spread on the melting the ice on our air and seaports, and all other roads and some alley-ways, for the continuation of the economy and our everyday activities. People to educate and train the Caribbean about all what to expect, what is needed, livestock's, Agriculture and farming, heating and the whole works that involves 'Snow falling' in hot climate countries and Islands during climate change. Then in the case of the 'Rising of the Seas' causing 'Tsunamis,' I suggested to both Prime Minister David Cameron and President Barack Obama, some of the things which needs to be in place in the Caribbean. People let me pause to inform you that President Barack Obama got his letter long before the Haiti disaster, so he were knowledgeable of what to expect . . . therefore Mr. President were fore-warned before it took place. People God loves us so much that before destructions He always sends us warnings! People God is good to us although we fails Him in numerous ways . . . give Him Thanks!

People, I am speaking about 2009—2010. I went a little further and suggests to both gentlemen that the Caribbean will be greatly in needs of Air Rescue Transports Operation in place, rescuing people from the seas and transporting them to U.K and USA. Therefore housing and shelter must be puts in place and all that involves in disasters preparation.

Some of the things needed in hot Climatic countries with the introduction of 'Snow' falling.

a) Every Country or Island needs a very large 'Budget,' very costly

b) New Price control.

c) Training and preparing the entire population, adapting to new system.

d) Teaching the population how to ski and enjoy the sport and fun in the snow.

e) People especially older, very young ones and low immune system . . . needs special help and medication getting adapt to new environment.

f) Heating and Cooling to; all living, working, recreation, environment for both man, animals and birds.

g) New introduction Constructions building Code in general accommodating both heating and cooling, special attention to all roofs . . . all galvanizing roof are band forever (enemy to snow and hails).

h) All Constructed homes and businesses needs a well-organized secured 'Basement' as a must because in the changing of this weather . . . Dangerous 'Tornadoes,' will be a part of the mixed in this climate change.

i) All Contactors too needs a crash course accommodating the new building Code . . . all roofs ceiling with fibre-glass.

j) The general public need a 'Government-Loan, interest free, with a grace period of one year . . . for the re-construction of their homes to accommodate the new system.

k) Agriculture, farming and livestock care and preparation . . . switching over will cause a big lost to a large percentage of our; Agriculture, farming and livestock's.

l) Heating and cooling for all vehicles; proper MOT (Road worthy) and tools for de-icing.

m) All Motor-mechanics needs a fresh crash course for switching-over.

n) Proper package of 'winter' outfits; clothing, shoes and general.

o) Equipment, tools and training, for spreading 'Salt' on all roads surfaces, special ones for air and sea-ports . . . the general public too must be knowledgeable of salt usage.

p) All children must be in school during school time and should not be found on the streets!

q) All Politicians, Police and Pastors and Army personals should be given the rightful permission to chastise, flog and taken to school, those children's and fine the parents . . . and the ling list goes on!

r) Finally, 'All' adults; Parents, Politicians, Teachers must be at church each Sunday with their families, Giving God Thanks and Praise, setting the stage, a sample of a good example to our children and future generations. This will eliminates more than half the problem in this world.

Jesus loves us, died for us and showing us how much He Loves us by giving us a warning, saying get ready, be prepared for this new change. What kind of change? Climate change from your warm nice comfortable oven-feeling into an icy cold deep freeze! Jesus is saying, that this earthly climate change are temporal but He is offering man an eternal climate change a place He has gone to prepare for mankind which is far better. Are you ready? If not get ready, while you have life and all your senses still intact, do the right thing, do it now! Open your heart and let Jesus in, because this can be His final call, knocking at your heart's door!

Let Him in, 'Jesus'!

He waits outside your Heart's Door,
Let Him in, 'Jesus,' before He departs,
TODAY can be His Last visit,
To return 'No More.'
He 'Loves' you!
He is 'The only Way, The Truth and Life Eternal'!
He died to save you!
He wants to Abide in your Heart,
He wants to give you Eternal Life,
Would you open your Heart's Door?
He's waiting for you to make your Choice.
Between Life and Death, Jesus said, 'Choose Life'!
As He gently knocks, let Him in, 'JESUS'!
Let the Saviour in!

Author John A Hodge.

MR. John A. Hodge,
28 Church Drive,
Carrington,
Nottingham,

NG5 2BA,
U. K.
16th April, 2010.

The Honourable,
Barack H. Obama,
President of the United States of America,
The White House,
1600 Pennsylvania Avenue,
Washington D.C.
United States of America.

Dear Mr. President,

Greetings again in Jesus Precious Name, out soon coming King, the one who reigns for ever and ever, Amen. As God continue to sustain life, I never cease praying for you, your family, the United States of America, Israel and the rest of the World.

Mr. President, my name is John A. Hodge. A servant of the Most High God, just doing the things He commands me to do.

Sir, this a recap of who is John A. Hodge. Last year around this time, The Lord God of Host gave me a revelation concerning the relationship of Israel and The United States of America. The ownership of Israel's inherited LAND. That is being fought over. Also God's choice of The United States of America, long before the World began.

In making reference to dramatic, frightening changing seasons of life, and the drama of endless trips to and from the drawing board trying to solve this climate change problem, this will make anyone instantly gray.

Mr. President, in making reference to the "rising of the sea level," and the damage it will do to man and his inhabitation. Naturally, man will be in great need, and all will be looking to you (Mr. President), like children looking to their daddy for help. I know that, as the President and one who is conscious of these changes to our climate, you do have a plan in place (machinery, food, clothing, shelter, water, medical help, and manpower, etc.).

Can I make few suggestions that can be added to your well organized list and plans? I suggest that you indicate to the top G-20 Countries. It is not too early to start building large warehouses and start storing excess food and grains, such as corn, wheat, peas, and other non-perishables. Naturally, there is going to be a famine; we will lack food and water. Also, excess shelter for long term housing of people, a reserve of manpower (both military and voluntary), and floating hospitals and hotels. There must be specially designed floating launch pads to rescue man from the sea. Also, large, floating sea rescue operation planes and helicopters. These are some of the things I suggest will be needed due to the rising sea level in the Caribbean and elsewhere.

Mr. President, my prayers are with you, your family, your cabinet, The United States of America, Israel, and the rest of the world. As I pray to God, I bring you to the throne of God's mercy seat, asking that God will bless you with the blessings of Jabez and the Wisdom of Solomon.

In closing, let these words of the Psalmist lift you and your family's spirits, which is taken from Psalm 4:3, "But know that the LORD hath set apart him that is godly for himself: the LORD will hear when I hear when I call upon him." In God we put our Eternal Trust.

Yours sincerely

Servant of the Most High God
John A. Hodge.

N. B.

Today is 31st July, 2015, sad to say this, but from the date of this letter, 16th April, 2010, until now, the 'World' have being experiencing; numerous disasters of all kind and type, millions of people are running for their live with their young children's, many a lives have being lost at sea as boats loads of people risking and fleeing for their lives, yet until 'NOW 'no actions has been taken! Such like building Large Warehouses, storing-up the goods etc. Presently, untold number of people are dying because of the lack of food and water. Famine has been here for a while now and I have seen no drastic action taken. Hello out there, is anybody listening? Does anybody really care? The people are crying out for help and they cannot do nothing else to help themselves. Our young babies are dying, the condition is too much and they cannot take it anymore! Where is our love for each other? We are all human! Is there compassion still alive? Church, I am speaking to you!

People, this is not the government's responsibility, No! Let us stop looking to government for everything, yes, they are doing a lot to help. Church, God said, this is your responsibility, showing, love, mercy and compassion to the poor, needy and destitute, by reaching out to them with physical and spiritual food! The Church has turn its backs and are continually running away from its true responsibility, so the government shows love and took up this task.

Today the government has more Love and compassion than the very church today! Church, where are you, stop dodging and hiding with your flimsy excuses! The government will not deny you help, but you are running from your responsibility, these people running with their children and drowning are not the government children, No! These needy people are your (The Church) children; supports them, look for them, feed them, clothes them, comfort and love them! Shame on you! Imagine the government in U.K., stretching out its hand and giving the church money! Shame on you! You should be the one giving to the government! Imagine the government, obediently honouring God and His Word, paying its rightful 'Tithes and Offering,' to the Lord! This is one of the reason United Kingdom is blessed, because God said, when you pay your 'Tithes and Offering,' He will BLESS YOU! God is keeping His promises, honouring His Holy Word and Blessing the United Kingdom!

Church, God said, this monies of Tithes and Offering, is to; pay the spiritual leaders, church maintenance, helping the poor and needy, the widows, the orphans and the list goes on! The government willingly and gladly doing more than its portion or more than enough, every day the government gets a new problem to deal with, quickly looking for solutions to solves its many problems and still find time and money dealing with your responsibility! This is not right nor is it fair to no government. It is more than high time for the 'CHURCH,' to stop its running and shoulders its true responsibilities. CHURCH, give the government a break and shoulders your jobs and duties!

The ones who are responsible for taking the leading role is the Church and not the government. The Church is the one with the power like the main generator giving or distributing 'Light,' to everyone, this too involves the government. If the power-source or generator (the Church), is not working or functioning properly that means it is darkness all around. If the Church is in darkness, this means that the government too is in darkness, because for the government to get light, it has to plug into the Church, the power-source or generator.

Church, where is you're 'Power,' giving light and taking the leading role directing traffic? The Church is quiet, sleeping, snoring and fast asleep! How can you be fast asleep and people are crying out in great need and you're not there, sounding your voice, even with a word of comfort. Church it is time to shine your 'Light,' the people are in darkness and want to see their way out. Arise from your sleep and slumber because Jesus who is 'Light' has given you that same 'Light.' As Brother of the Son of man, rise up O man of God' and make the Church great! The Psalmist written in Psalm: 133, reads, 'Behold, how good and pleasant it is for brethren to dwell together in unity! It is like the precious ointment upon the head, that ran down upon the beard, even Aaron's beard: that went down to the skirts of his garments; As the dew of Hermon, and as the dew that descended upon the mountains of Zion: for there the Lord commanded the blessing, even life for evermore.'

A Heart of Love.

Is there any 'LOVE,' in our Hearts to quickly forgive?

Is there any 'LOVE,' in our Hearts to tenderly embrace our stubborn enemies?

Is there any 'LOVE,' in our Hearts to voluntarily give a helping hand?

Is there any 'LOVE,' in our Hearts to gladly render good for evil?

Is there any 'LOVE,' in our Hearts to willingly and gladly show mercy?

Is there any 'LOVE,' in our Hearts to patiently reach out to the needy?

Is there any 'LOVE,' in our Hearts to truly for 'All Men Everywhere';

In spite of 'Race, Colour, Language or Creed?

God who is 'LOVE,' has being offended by man,

Yet His 'LOVE,' remains the same.

If we are followers of God, 'Yes' we too can do likewise.

LOVE is a 'Healer'; it has the Power to heal!

It has the Power to heal 'ALL WOUNDS,' which is caused by the hatred of men,

LOVE is the only conqueror, which conquerors everything that is apply to life and living!

A Heart of 'LOVE.'

Author John A. Hodge.

THIS IS A DREAM, THE REVELATION OF TSUNAMIS IN THE CARIBBEAN.

Urgent Emergency! Respond now!
Address,
The Lord Jesus Christ,
He is the Way,
He is the Truth,
He is Life Eternal,
Telephone #
Emergency 911 (Prayer).

Dear Caribbean People,

Greetings to you in the Wonderful and Powerful Name of Jesus, our soon coming King, grace, mercy, peace and Love is your 'hedge of protection.'

My name is John A Hodge, a proud National of St. Kitts, with Anguillian heritage and roots. I am a born again, blood wash child of God. At present I am residing here in England.

My true purpose in life is to fully dedicate in doing the 'Will of God,' and to faithfully fulfil His desires, plans and purposes for my life as He so choses.

My Caribbean people, I do not have the time for more details, due to the urgency of the matter I am going to deal with now.

God is loving, kind, gracious and faithful to all men in spite of our unthankfulness to Him, as He continues to bless us with life day by day. This is proof of a loving God displaying His merciful kindness towards us.

God is angry and unhappy with us (Caribbean people), and before judgment and destruction, God always sends a clear warning. Let us be reminded of these words which is so true, 'Where there is no VISION, the people perish. So let us be thankful to God for His voice of VISION. In this VISION, God is simply saying to us, the choice is ours/yours, choose your destination, life or death.' 'NOW'!

The children of Israel too had this same chance to choose. They went astray doing their own thing, serving strange gods and idols which makes God angry. Then God spoke to them through His Prophet Joshua, who addressed the people. They were encouraged by the Prophet Joshua to choose life. Obediently, they heeded Joshua's choice and chose "Life." In doing so, they said to Joshua, "And the people said unto Joshua, The Lord our God will we serve, and his voice we will obey" (Josh. 24:24)

So my dear Caribbean people, I am here encouraging you too to do like-wise, "choose life!" And in doing so we will all receive the Benefits and Blessings in choosing "life."

My dear Caribbean people for a very long time, God has being speaking and revealing Himself to me on countless times and numerous ways. Today I want to tell you God is real, and just as He has spoken to His Prophets in the past, He is still doing the same today. My God never change, He remains the same, He is the God of Yesterday, Today and Forever, He changed not'!

I am not trying to jump ahead, doing my own thing or to do and say things to be seen and heard of men. No! What I am doing and saying is all by the command of God-Himself.

God for a long time is constantly speaking to me and directing me in areas of prayer, with a 'Word' for someone and also to bless others.

I am now aware and understanding what Moses other Prophets, Servants and <u>Shepherds</u> whom God has chosen to fulfil a special task as He commands them.

Moses questioned God, asking, "Who shall I say sent me?" Then, God said unto Moses, "I AM, that I AM sent me unto you!"

I am not ashamed to say, I too asked God this same question, I know God is speaking to me and He gave me a command. So I asked God, 'What shall I say to these people in order for them to know and believe I am sent by you? Because I am afraid and timid.

Then God replied to me through His Holy Word. God The Holy Spirit led me to Philippians 4:9, in which He clearly said to me, **"Those things, which ye have both learned and received, and heard, and seen in me, do, and the God of peace shall be with you."**

Although I got the approval of His Command, I still allowed fear to with-held me. Then God who knows and sees our heart, saw the fear, then finally led me to 1 John 4:18, where He finally spoke to me and said, 'There is no fear in love, but perfect love casteth out fear; because fear hath torment. He that feareth is not made perfect in love.' Do what I commanded you to do in love and have No FEAR!

My Caribbean people, I found myself dreaming every night which started the first week of November, 2009. And in all these dreams every night I saw the 'SEA,' in its anger and furry also people and other activities taking place. I saw at one time the 'SEA,' rough and people swimming and struggling to reach land. In another dream, I saw the 'SEA' rough and houses been swallowed up by it. Another time I saw dead bodies including little babies under the water alive reaching out their little hands for someone to help them. Also I saw people walking and playing in the 'SEA.' I then got concerned and prayed to God, asking Him to clearly show me what He is saying to me concerning the 'SEA.'

My dear Caribbean people, God answers all prayers. Sometimes He says YES! Another time His answers, saying No! Also at time He will say, Wait! As human when we pray to God the only answer we know of is 'Yes' and this often get us into serious trouble or a dis-agreement with God, who is Just, Holy, Right and Righteous.

Then after praying that night, in a dream, God took me to the place of my birth (St. Kitts), Leeward Island, West Indies and made the VISION clear to me. God clearly showed me the presence of a tsunami, in St. Kitts and the entire Caribbean.

People allows me to share with you a glimpse of what I saw. I found myself in a house in St. Kitts. This dwelling two story-house were constructed on a hill, with a good landscaping drainage, impossible for water to settle on the land. This house was built approximately seven hundred feet away from the cliff that bordered the SEA. Also, this cliff had a 70–80 ft. drop to the shores of the SEA.

In this dream, I was on the top floor. Then stepping out of the house onto the platform or veranda, I then started to descend. Looking down I saw water settled in the yard or lawn, which I knew were impossible because of the drainage of the land-scape. Quickly I questioned myself of this impossible situation, then suddenly raising my head and looking off, the sight I saw, almost cause my heart to leaped out of my trembling body.

In looking up I saw the Wide-Vast-Blue-Ocean stood in front of me overflowing the 70–80 feet cliff/hill, overflowing the entire yard and beyond.

Only then I understood clearly what God is saying to me, in those dreams, concerning the SEAS in the Caribbean.

God showed me the expectation of a tsunami in the Caribbean. He clearly showed me the SEAS, rising to an impossible level, which will be hard for men to believe. Also this rising of the NEW SEA LEVEL, remained permanent. This clearly showed that the main based of the entire Island of St. Kitts and all the low land of the entire Caribbean were underwater covered by the rising SEAS. Imagine the great loss of lives of both people, animals and properties swallowed up and buried in the SEAS, caused by this tsunami.

People of the Caribbean God loves us still although we are not trusting, worshipping and serving Him as we should. Although we have pushed Him out of our lives, His Unconditional Love for us remains the same. Jesus loves us, died for us, yet we are still trampling on His precious blood, He shed for all our sins. This expected 'Tsunami' is withheld for many years, through a lot of prayers by faithful Christians seeking God face on a daily basis of behalf of unthankful Caribbean people. This 'Tsunami' is indeed a warning to us from a Loving God! Are we ready to take heed and respond to His merciful-kindness towards us?

ANOTHER DREAM CONCERNING CARIBBEAN PEOPLE.

People let me share with you another dream the Lord God showed me over 35 years ago, concerning the state of the Caribbean and all its inhabitations. Caribbean people we are in serious trouble with God for a very long time and we are only surviving through His constant 'Tender Mercy' on us. How long will God extend His Love and mercy towards us, when we are ignorant, wilful and shows we do not care?

Caribbean people allows me to pause and share this another dream with you. In this dream, over 35 years ago, the Lord God showed me where the SEAS, covered the entire inhabitation of the whole Caribbean leaving only the pinnacles of the highest mountains of the whole Caribbean to be seen.

God took me up to the top of one of the highest mountain in the Caribbean, and said unto me, look down! In looking down from the pinnacle of this mountain, I saw the sight of a deep precipice below and everything swallowed up and covered by the, ENTIRE SEAS, except the pinnacles of the highest mountains emerging above. There was no sight of man, land, houses, animals, or trees; there was nothing but the "Vast-Wide-Beep-Blue-Ocean-Of-Seas." The total Caribbean vanished and disappeared. There were no more Caribbean, it was covered by the SEAS!

My Caribbean I am not trying to scare anyone, but just sharing with you a glimpse of what I saw in these dreams, as I compare these two dreams concerning the Caribbean. I, John, saw these things which are to come if we fail to turn from our wicked ways and serve the true and Living God, who in His Everlasting Merciful-Kindness, is waiting to hear from us. We are going to feel and experience the full furry of God's wrath. God can and will show His Mercy on us by turning this physical tsunami into a spiritual tsunami, sweeping the whole Caribbean, again if we turn from serving these strange gods and idols, confessing our sins and asking God to reaches out to us with His Hands of Mercy.

My Caribbean people, God is angry with us from turning our backs on Him, serving strange gods and idols. The gods of obeah, negamancy, witchcraft, voodoo, self, pride, materialism, and success. God the Holy Spirit said, "Not only Caribbean people, proudly worshipping and serving strange gods and idols, but they are proudly and fiercely teaching it to their children and grandchildren. They are destroying future generations and denying them the experience of knowing the REAL POWER of the True and Living God. Caribbean people God is angry with us and is sending us this 'Warning before Destruction'!

My Caribbean people, when God showed me the revelation of the tsunami in the Caribbean, the first thing I did was to pray about the whole matter. Next I called my spiritual father, Pastor Gladstone Hazel, St. Thomas, USVI, I shared with him the dream, after we prayed in agreement (this were his suggestion), that God would show His mercy on us (Caribbean people). Also I called a few Pastors including the late Pastor Stanley Edwards, and others in St. Kitts, who also prayed and continued for a while. I finally told my Spiritual father that God commanded me to warn the people, so he encouraged me to pursue. People these dreams started in the first week of November, 2009, and continued for a while until the end of February, 2010. I kept most of these dreams to myself. I got a break but then on 1st April, 2010, it came back again and lasted until 17th April, 2010. God brought it back because He wanted me to warn the people.

People, these dreams are not ordinary dreams, Oh no! So I am encouraging you to; Stop, Look, Listen, Take Heed and Obey, Now! Choose Life and Live!

Caribbean people, we cannot fool God because he is the only Creator. We are not fooling Satan because he is the Father of Lies. We cannot fool ourselves because we know the truth of the whole matter. In Psalm 44:22, we are reminded who God is, "Shall not God search this out? For He knoweth the secrets of the heart?"

My dear Caribbean people, God wants us to destroys and get rid of all the books, symbols, pictures, music, crystal balls, and artefacts that are associated with these gods and idols (Especially Christians) now. He wants us to confess our sins from our hearts and life. Also, teach it to our children, grandchildren, and future generations. In Romans 10:9–10, we read, "That if thou shalt confess with thy mouth the Lord Jesus, and shalt believe in thine heart that God hath raised Him from the dead, thou shalt be saved, 'For with the heart man believeth unto righteousness; and with the mouth confession is made unto salvation.'"

THIS NEXT DREAM IS ABOUT THE REVELATION OF THE RAPTURE (SUPERNATURAL REVELATION).

A Large percentage of Christians, pastors, theologians, Bible teachers, and evangelists do not believe in the Rapture. It is said the word Rapture is not in the Bible. The words and phrases which most describes the Rapture, are words like caught-up in the air, snatched, caught away, to carry off, and to catch up.

Having a dream of the Rapture is indeed God Manifested Revelation. Only certain people, according to God standard of righteousness, are qualified to have sacred hidden things revealed to them.

13 But I would not have you to be ignorant, brethren, concerning them which are asleep, that ye sorrow not, even as others which have no hope.

14 For if we believe that Jesus died and rose again, even so them also which sleep in Jesus will God bring with him.

15 For this we say unto you by the word of the Lord, that we which are alive and remain unto the coming of the Lord shall not prevent them which are asleep.

16 For the Lord himself shall descend from heaven with a shout, with the voice of the archangel, and with the trump of God: and the dead in Christ shall rise first:

[17]Then we which are alive and remain shall be caught up together with them in the clouds, to meet the Lord in the air: and so shall we ever be with the Lord.
[18]Wherefore comfort one another with these words.
1 Thessalonians 4:13–18.

Today many people are confused about the 'Rapture,' and confusing themselves by asking all kind of questions, such as; what time it will take place, would it take place before the Great Tribulation, in the middle of the Great Tribulation or at the end of the Great Tribulation? Some go so far as to say that they do not believe this will ever take place because in the Bible/Scriptures the word 'Rapture' cannot be found or it is not recorded but they all agreed that a number of phrases and words recorded in the Bible/Scriptures are related to the 'Rapture.' Imagine a large percentage of these same people are; Spiritual-leaders, Pastors, Evangelists, Ministers and Teachers of the Word of God and the list goes on. These Spiritual-leaders are ignorant confused people and they are teaching and preaching their opinion of ignorance, finally confusing their congregations, then their congregations become just like them ignorant and confuse.

A lot of these spiritual leaders are reading the Word of God preaching and teaching their own opinion and confusing the people, who are looking to them for Spiritual guidance . . . Most of these so-called Spiritual-leaders do not have no relationship with God and to be intimate with God one must have a relationship with Him. Therefore, God the Holy Spirit is a total stranger and foreigner to them, there's no communication whatsoever. Do these people meditate on the Word that they preach, teach and evangelized? We have been hearing is that the blind leading the blind all falling into the ditch, with their 20 twenty vision physically operating well but spiritually blind. 'And Philip ran thither to him, and heard him read the prophet Esaias, and said, Understandest thou what thou readest? And he said,

How can I except some man should guide me? And he desired that he would come up and sit with him,'

Long before birth was given to me, God had chosen me and assigned me to this task, bearing this message the Revelation of 'Rapture' to this confused people of this world. The Rapture is the second coming of Jesus, fulfilling His promise to us. John 14:3 reads, "And if I go and prepare a place for you, I will come again, and receive you unto myself; that where I am, there ye may be also."

People allows me to share with you one more dream, God entrusted me with approximately fifteen years ago. I will be brief. This dream is the Revelation of the Rapture, which is so important to all children of the Most High God. This will bring closure of comfort, joy, assurance, satisfaction, and a great sense of relief of a confused mind.

In this world in which we are living for many years, many thousands or should I say millions of women got pregnant at some stage and were not aware that they were pregnant. Some discovered their state of pregnancy after a period of three months, some find out five or six months later and others never find out until they gave birth to a full term nine month's pregnancy, the birth of a healthy 'Baby.' All mothers knows the special, precious, uniqueness of a new born baby, they are blessings and gifts of love from God.

For many years I've been busy doing all kind of things and were not aware like so many women I am pregnant with historical record of carrying multi-precious babies and presently at the stage of delivery. I am now fully matured and knowledgeable of the Precious Blessings and the gifts of love God entrusted to my care. Like my namesake, John the Revelatory, who wrote the last book of the Bible (Revelations), revealing to the world the Revelations of the hidden and secrets things concerning the last days.

People God the Holy Spirit blessed me with a double blessings, in the revelation of the Rapture, to deliver to this world. God gave me this same identical vision of the Rapture, twice in a time span of 2 years.

In this identical glimpse of the 'Rapture,' was similar to that which John saw when he was caught-up in the 'Spirit of God,' on the Isle of Patmos, when he wrote the Book of Revelation, which is the Revelation of Jesus Christ. In this dream, the sky was bright with the Glory of God. I believe this brightness was equal the same experience Moses spoke of when he spent forty days and forty nights in the presence of God at Mount Sinai, where he received the 10 Commandments on stone tablets. The Bible said, as he returned to the children of Israel, his face shone so bright, he had to put a veil on his face because the children of Israel were unable to withstand it's reflected the Shekinah Glory Of God. King Solomon too had that same experience when he had the Dedication of the Temple. In this dream, I experienced the whole place lit with the presence of His Shekinah's Glory. The skies were jam-packed with Christians, children, saints, and elects of God. There were multitudes of people as far as eyes can see, all on bended knees around Jesus in a circle. We were all in mid-air, kneeling on bended knees with Jesus standing in the middle, with His hands at His side. Jesus, the son of God and the saviour of the world, stood erect and silent. He said not a word! People if a pin had dropped with such Throng/Multitude of people, it would had sounded like an earthquake because of the blessed-quietness. JESUS' face shone so brightly that no one could have identified any part of His Face. It was like a bright light bulb giving off its rays of light, too bright for the human eyes, but you knew His head was on His body.

Then all of us started to sing in Unison the hymn, "Lamb of god our souls adore thee, while upon thy face we gaze, there the father love and mercy, shining in all their brightest rays, thine almighty power and wisdom all creation works proclaim, heaven and earth alike confess thee, as the ever great I am." We sung all four verses, looking stead-fast upon His Face, at His Feet, on bended knees in mid-air, with all our tears flowing like a river. We gave Him all of our Honour, Praise, Worship, and Glorified His Name. We gave Him THANKS, because He is WORTHY and WORTHY of being PRAISED FOREVER! JESUS OUR LOVING SAVIOUR, stood in the Midst/Middle with

His hands at His side, just receiving all His children tributes to Him. He said, not a word!

World, people, the atmosphere were such no one can find words to describe it . . . it was indescribable. We were in a different world, a different place—it was Heaven in the air!

During such an indescribable atmospheric moment, I, John Adolphus Hodge, did not want to leave. I wanted to stay in that setting with all the Saints and Our Dear Loving Saviour and continues worshipping Him Forever! I did not want to come back to earth at all on those two occasion! But I now realized that God just wanted to give me a glimpse of what it is like to be in His presence Face to Face. He sent me back because He knew my task on earth was incomplete. This is part of His; Will, Plan and Purpose for me life, to get these messages, warnings and revelations to earth's populations.

Christians and none Christians, my message to you is simple, make sure you are truly serving and worshipping my true and living God because if you miss 'HEAVEN' you surely missed it all. From those two session in His Glorious presence, 'THINGS ON EARTH' mean nothing to me, I've often uses this phrase to many people, they may think it's just words of emptiness, they do not know but they are 'Words' from every mechanism of every cell in my entire body! All the wealth, riches, fame, fortune they are all vanity comparing to be in His presence! I've often told my two children Lynelle and Tristan Hodge, most of the proceeds of these books are going to do three things, it is my heart's desires and I knows fully well this is also my/our mother's heart's desires as well. A) Helping and blessing the needy. B) Helping to promote and spreading the Word of God. C) Encourages school children to 'Memorize' the scriptures, rewarding them with a monetary/financial gift . . . praying that God will speak to them through His Word to trust and know Him as He wants us to know Him fully.

Finally people Jesus is coming prepares to meet my God through His Son Jesus. Is He your God? If not, give Jesus your heart 'Now'! Tomorrow might be too late! He said, come 'Now' and let us reason together He loves you, He came to saves you and He died for you! He was ascended into heaven to prepare a place for you! His return can be any moment, the signs are clear for all to see, again trust Him 'Now'! You have nothing to lose but heaven to gain!

CAN ANY MAN SEE GOD FACE TO FACE AND LIVE? THE ANSWER IS . . . NO!

In life some people are reading the Bible/Scriptures and are a bit confused of some passages of scriptures that is read. Then some wisely visit a place of worship seeking help from either the Spiritual-leader of the church or and approachable member of that church. Also instead of getting help, these people finds themselves much more confused asking questions seeking help, because some of whom these questions are directed to, at times they themselves do not know the answers to these because of numerous reasons. Today some people go to church listened the preached sermon, sits in a Sunday school class and never do a research to find out and to see for themselves if what is said is really so . . . these days a lot of those who delivers the Word of God quotes from their own opinion and few reference to the scriptures that is read. This is why we needs to research the Word for ourselves for a better understanding of what the scriptures says. Then another group would not even pick up the Bible and read not even a verse of scripture for themselves for Spiritual guidance for their day. Some delights to quotes what the Pastor said and that's it, as if the Pastor is a book of the Bible. People Pastor is much happier when everyone can look at the scriptures for themselves and be of some help to Him, new members who are looking for help and guidance. This is helping him, giving him a sense of satisfaction knowing you are making yourself available to help when there is a need.

People are willing to learn, and in doing so a lot of questions are going to be directed to those they feels should have the answers, moreover if that one is a foundation member of that church. Christians needs to be equipped, ready and willing to answer some of these questions that some people asks. As Christians we are encouraged to study the Word in season and out of season, this means there is no season to rest from studying the Word. In doing so as a member you are making your Pastor feeling rather proud, with the realization that his work in not in vain because of the positive growth of such members.

This topic is a question that is confusing a lot of people's minds and causing a great deal of contradictions in a large percentage of churches today even among many Pastors. There are more questions asked by people outside of the church and little or no answers is given in reply! This is poor results and a bad reflection on any church. Let's assumed a member of the public choose to ask you this question which is troubling a lot of Christians and Spiritual leaders today. Can anyone see God's face and live? What would you do or what will your answer be? Are you going to give an excuse to get off the hook or run calling your, Sunday school teacher, a long-time foundation member or disturbing your Pastor's appointment?

Although some Spiritual leader are serving for donkey years, this do not say they have the answers to all questions asked. No! The Bible is a large book and each passage of scriptures needs time to; read, meditates on, searching more scriptures for some clarity on the first scripture, many prayers about the passage seeking the help and guidance of God the Holy Spirit for answers, at times one have to apply a special time of Prayer and Fasting seeking the heart and mind of God's manifestations and revelations, sometimes a Bible study is required with either other Spiritual leaders or even some church foundation mature members. Why? Because several heads are better that one and one member may have had a 'Revelation from God the Holy Spirit,' on this topic or subject matter in the past but never did had the opportunity to share it with no one.

This question gave and is still giving everyone the same headaches in coming up with the right answer convincing everyone it is the truth and the whole-truth. This question has caused many arguments and falling-out among many Bible theologians, because none decides to accept either opinions. And today a large percentage of Spiritual leaders are hoping no one confronts them with it. Spiritual leaders are too; big-headed, stubborn like a mule, full of self-pride like a peacock, arrogant and ignorant, just to humble ones selves, coming down off your high horse, by simply saying, 'Sorry I do not know the answer, but I will do a research on it and get back to you on it!

In the Bible we can read of Prophets and others who came close to God, spoke face to face with Him, 'But They Never Did Literally Saw His (God's) Face. Now I understand how this were done. Moses spoke to God face to face, at Mount Sinai, when he got the 10 Commandments. King Solomon too came close, at the dedication of the Temple, but never saw God's face literally! Jacob gave account of seen God face to face but he too, did not see God's literal or physical face. Then you may ask, what about Adan and Eve, they has sweet fellowship with God face to face, didn't they saw God's face to face? Adam and Eve, did had sweet fellowship with God, but like all those men we spoke of, who confessed to spoke to God and saw His face, they (Adam and Eve) too never saw God's literal/ physical face!

Titus 1:2 reads, "In hope of eternal life, which God, that cannot lie, promised before the world began"; People we are speaking about 'God,' the only 'Creator' of everything! The only One who is; Perfect, Pure, Holy, Righteous and always 'Right'! GOD, 'CANNOT LIE AND WILL NOT LIE'! Are we trying to trap God, the one who created us, knows our hearts and knows us long before He Created heaven and earth? God said, 'There Shall No Man See Me and Live'! All who confessed to saw God's face, did not saw God's literal/physical face, No! What they all saw was the image likened that of a man, from His neck down to His feet. What did they see then? They saw the covering of His face, which is the Shekinah's Glory. That big bright diamond-like sparkling spot-light, that which no man natural eyes can with-stand of pierced! So how can man's eyes see His Face? Impossible for any to see God's face and live! This is what I saw in those dreams: the Revelation of the Rapture!

Moses was in the presence of God for forty days and forty nights, speaking to Him face to face, as they spoke about the 10

Commandments, which Moses took to the camp of the children of Israel. Moses did not saw His literal/physical face, but the 'Brightness of God's Glory or the Shekinah's Glory of God. Moses could not identify neither His; Eyes, Mouth, Nose, Ears, Chine or His Jaws, No! Just spending that amount of time in God's presence for forty days and forty nights, the Brightness of His Face (Shekinah's Glory) shone so bright that it actually leaves that; illumination, it's glow, brightness, sparkling-radiation were imprinted on the face of Moses, that he (Moses) had to covered his face in order to speak to the children of Israel, because his face too shone with the same imprints of Shekinah's Glory on his face.

When one spends time in the presence of God in; prayer, praise and worship, prayer and fasting, seeking His face, having sweet fellowship with Him, it is a fact that evidence will always appears or showing itself even without any question asked. Everyone will know that that person have an intimate relationship with God.

Exodus: 33: 17—20, reads, And the LORD said unto Moses, I will do this thing also that thou hast spoken: for thou hast found grace in my sight, and I know thee by name.

[18] And he said, I beseech thee, shew me thy glory.

[19] And he said, I will make all my goodness pass before thee, and I will proclaim the name of the LORD before thee; and will be gracious to whom I will be gracious, and will shew mercy on whom I will shew mercy.

[20] And he said, Thou canst not see my face: for there shall no man see me, and live.

Exodus 33:11 reads, "And the Lord spake unto Moses face to face, as a man speaketh unto his friend, And he turneth again into the camp: but his servant Joshua, the son of Nun, a young man, departed not out of the tabernacle."

Genesis 32:30 reads, "And Jacob called the name of the place Peniel: for I have seen God face to face, and my life is preserved."

John 1:18 reads, "No man hath seen God at any time, the only begotten Son, which is in the bosom of the Father, he hath declared him."

1 John 4:12 reads, "No man hath seen God at any time. If we love one another, God dwelleth in us, and his love is perfected in us."

COPENHAGEN. THE TOWER OF BABEL DECEMBER, 2009.

G od who is all powerful, omnipotent, omnipresence, and omniscience is still in full controls of everything both in heaven
and on earth.

God in His Holy Word continues to speak to man in numerous
ways, saying love and worship the Lord thy God! Love one another,
and live peaceable with all men. God is simply saying to live in
'UNITY'! Yet as mankind, we fail to take heed to God's Word and
command to us.

Unity is Oneness! Unity is Strength! Unity is Love! Unity is
Power! Unity is Victory and Unity is God!

The Psalmist reminds us in Psalm 127:1, "Except the Lord build
the house, they labour in vain that build it: except the Lord keep the
city, the watchman walketh but in vain!"

The Psalmist is telling mankind, and the 192 Nations repre-
sented at the 2009 United Nations Climate Change Conference in
Copenhagen, Denmark, to reach an agreement concerning climate
change. Our reliance on God is a far more important than a conference if we expects positive answers and results.

At this conference, words like these were uttered, "Copenhagen
is a good opportunity and right time for the World to agree on
Climate deal which could save earth's planet from catastrophic climate change." Also, "Climate concerns, is falling away and continues to fall from the interest of man." As words continued to flow,
we read "This matter is difficult, and we expects difficult results

and decisions." Men continued to get a little nervous and confused, resulting in words like these, "time is running out, the world is looking on, remember the power of the pen is going to write the history of the outcome of this important topic."

At the UN's Copenhagen Conference, world leaders were urged in advance to "unite" and reach a good workable deal on climate change.

The conclusion reminds us of the building of the TOWER OF BABEL, which ends because of man's lack of obedience to God's command. This action provoked God to create a barrier of misunderstanding, unity, and language communication skills. He put a stop order on the completion of man's bright idea of building a skyscraper to heaven.

The answer to and results of climate change are indeed outside of the reach and boundary of man's best technology. So all we need to do is give God the creator an invitation, pray for wisdom, knowledge, and understanding, and let Him guide us in solving our problem.

THE ENTIRE EARTH WILL BE PLUNGING INTO UTTER DARKNESS.

During my early teens, I can clearly recall a gentleman by the name of Andrea, who lived in the capital (Basseterre) of St. Kitts. Andrea walked the streets with a big school bell, approximately three or four days weekly. For hours, he rang that bell at intervals, shouting at the top of his voice, saying, "Perilous days are coming!" People would usually come out of their homes and workplaces to look at him as he gave that warning to all the people living in that area. I cannot recall how far he went outside of Basseterre in St. Kitts, ringing that bell of warning, reminding the people of the days which are now here.

Later in my youth, I realized he was indeed a messenger of God, a prophet, sent by God, with a simple message of warning to the people. He was like John the Baptist, saying, "repent and be baptised for the forgiveness of your sins, for the kingdom of heaven is near." God speaks to mankind every day and God always has a man, a messenger, or a prophet prepared to send to the people with a special message: a word of warning for that time, era, and season, before every judgment day. Isaiah 50:4 reads, "The Lord God hath given me the tongue of the learned, that I should know how to speak a word in season to him that is weary: he waketh morning by morning, he waketh mine ear to hear as the learned." This is another season, time, and era and God has chosen, called and has sent me with this

Word for you the people of the entire world, saying, "prepare yourself, get ready, trust Jesus as your Saviour, let Him controls your life and escapes the wrath of God which is to come, the awful judgment day because Jesus is coming soon." We are presently living in the same perilous days, which Andrea, the messenger and Prophet of God spoke of decades ago.

The entire earth and the world population are presently experiencing climate change that no one can find a solution for. Therefore, during this new climate change, a lot of changes are going to take place, affecting nature all over the entire world until the coming of Jesus returning to this sinful world.

In one of these many dream of revelations, God the Father told me, "The entire earth will be plunged into a world of utter darkness." How soon this will take place and for how long will it last? I do not know, but just prepares yourself! Again, God always sends a messenger, with the Word of warning before the time of judgment day. People living in utter darkness for any period of time are experiencing judgment. In this dream, the Lord God said, before this experience of utter darkness, the moon will be going through a period of uncommon dramatic displays, something similar like the Eclipse we have seen twice this year (2015). The total Solar Eclipse on 20th March, total Lunar Eclipse on 4th April and hopefully the Partial Solar Eclipse on 13th September and Total Lunar Eclipse on 28th September. So the Moon will be doing strange things, similar to what we know, and it will be doing more new things which we have never experienced before. People during those Eclipse we have witness over the years, everyone did not experience the same effects, depends on where one lived on the face of the earth. In Nottingham, and many areas of UK and further beyond, some people experienced, heavy rain fall, strong stormy wind, dreadful coldness, darkness, hail stones falling and the list goes on. Here in Nottingham, I remembered the after effects almost two weeks after, the atmosphere and surroundings had a continued coldness that lingered on for a while. Everyone had their own different experienced that they can speak of.

During this new experience of utter darkness experience, the moon will be actively doing numerous quick constant tricks, which will get the attention of every human being living on the entire face of the earth. Everyone will be spell-bound asking questions and receiving little or no answers whatsoever, everyone will be always gazing upwards having their own opinions, fears and nervousness will all be out of controls. The place will be darken, the satellite system will be cut off and almost every communication system will be greatly affected, phones, radios, TV and the airborne communications system like the aeroplanes. Aeroplanes will be tumbling out of the skies and crashing because of the failing communications systems making the controls tower ineffective. All these different storms will be operating almost at the same time, boulders of ice will be crashing down on earth, dangerous tornadoes, blizzards of snow storms, none stop rain, and dead coldness, earthquakes and high tidal waves converting into Tsunami's . . . these are some of the earth's new experiences. We can just think of people living in hot climatic countries and islands and have to experience all these out of controlled acts of nature. What will be the reaction of these people who are unprepared for such a test? Would they be able to withstand such test of times? What would be the mental states of these people minds? How prepared are all these Countries, Islands and Nations, handling this kind of disasters? People, this is the warning voice of God to you, saying be prepared because perilous days are here! It is the voice saying to all ruling governments and all politicians to stop all these petty bickering and unite as one; Unity is Strength, Unity is Oneness, Unity is Power and Unity is Love . . . be prepared for the coming test, 'The plunging of the earth into Utter Darkness.' Who knows, a country or an Island in a hot Climatic area can experience a 'Blizzard of Snow Storm covering and burying the entire Island and that's it! We are going to experience things way-out-of-control of man.

For many years, we continue to hear that Jesus is coming. Some do not believe, but whether you believe or not, His coming is true and nearer than our belief. What more are we asking for? All these are signs of His soon returns to earth! All these warnings are saying, 'People love one another and prepares to meet the King of kings and Lord of lords.

People We Are All One.

It matters not if we are:
Black, white, yellow, purple, Chinese, Indian, Iraqi, Asian, or green,
Race, language, colour, or creed,
As human we are all one, and nothing can change our family!
God created one man and one woman!
He created Adam and Eve, from the dust of the earth!
What was their Colour, was it black, white, yellow or green?
They bore children, a reminder of Cain who slew his brother Abel!
And what was the colour of their Blood? 'Red! Red! Red'!

From Adam and Eve, the human race continues until 'NOW'!
Can you honestly tell me the answer to these questions?
What are we 'Fighting' for?
Why are we segregated?
And what is our alienation all about?
LET US LOVE ONE ANOTHER!
People we are ALL ONE!
One God!
One People!
One LOVE!

Author John A. Hodge

GREAT BRITAIN TO BE EXPERIENCING 'EARTHQUAKES' LIKE NEVER BEFORE.

During the period of these dreams, the Lord gave me a revelation of 'Destructive Earthquakes' that Great Britain will be experiencing which will draws world attention because of the vast devastation and the unbelievable trails of destructiveness involves. These 'Earthquakes' will be far exceeding the worst every historically recorded that Great Britain ever experienced, or should I say 'like never before.'

This period of these 'Destructive Earthquakes' will be of such great magnitude that the journalists and reporters will be mute, spellbound, appears to be dumb all gasping and grasping for words and voices as they tries to, reports and demonstrates the beholding of their sights. I do not know how soon this will take place, nor how much times it will struck, neither do I know how long each rumble will last nor the great destructions it will do to; England, Wales, Scotland, Ireland or Northern Ireland and the neighbouring EU countries. People, we have all our gas, electricity, water and cable-lines running underground and having such magnitude of 'Earthquakes' just imagine the chaos taking place. Also viewing from the sky the mapping, laying-out and architectural setting of all these millions of close-build houses with such big quakes, collapsing and crumbling of these houses . . . our streets and foot-paths will be totally blocked, leaving no room for manoeuvrings and escaping. This will be viewing of people trapped like fishes caught in nets fighting for their lives seeking help. Just looking at this terrifying situation, people trapped with little or no way of escaping, the water lines breaks adding to the misery of flooding the entire place. The gas lines exploring creating a blaze of fire with billows of black rising smoke, communication little or none whatsoever and the loud languishing screams like none stop sirens continues.

Having such destructions government will be facing with more challenges that they have never planned for, seeking the best solutions, solving their escalating problems. Needs arising for voluntary man-power both from the army, public and private sector. Medical personals of Doctors, Nurse, Technicians, and all volunteers in these areas. Helicopters, trained pilots, all building trades, building materials, building trades' men and the long lists go on.

Also Nottingham, are famously known for its endless underground caves and tunnels, with large-building erected structures sitting on top. Not forgetting the famous historian Robin Hood his Castle and underground 1426 structure escape tunnels. My questions are; what will manifests in these situations? Will those caves and tunnels structurally strong enough to withstand these testing periods of quakes and constant tremors, or would they collapse?

I am writing about all these revelations and sharing them with you, all residents of Great Britain, and the world at large to give you a preview or knowledge of what is to come. A few years ago, a letter was written and sent to those who have great concerns and are greatly involved in climate change, as well as to those in authority. The letter gave them first-hand knowledge of what to expect, sharing with them the revelations of these destructive earthquakes and everything that is to come. I also gave my ideas and suggestions concerning the urgency of early preparations for these dreadful periods. Within these letters, I vividly highlighted that we are heading for a serious famine and the urgent need to build large warehouses and store non-perishable foods. Letters were sent to a number of the heads of governments and also some churches. This is a list of some of the people letters were sent to: The President of the United States of America, the four living former presidents of USA, former Vice President Al Gore, both some Democrats and Republicans running for president, Great

Britain's Prime Minister and Deputy, the opposition leader, former Prime Minister Tony Blair, the Queen, the Prince of Wales, the Duke of Cambridge, the Prime Minister of St. Christopher/Nevis, as well as other heads of governments and church leaders.

People all these 'Revelations' the Lord entrusted me with, every one of them have to do with climate change. The entire earth is fully pregnant and have reached the stage, turning-point or should I say its mature limitation and presently at the stage or point of travailing, getting ready for its rebirth. Climate change is the reason for all these chains of earthquakes, the constant eruption of volcanoes vomiting their lava, the escalation of so many wars, the countless deaths of people fleeing for their lives, starvation, hurricanes, and sea levels rising in Europe like never before. Soon, the seas will turn black, the entire world will be plunged into total darkness, snow will fall in the Caribbean and other warm climates, sea levels will continue to rise, and deadly tsunamis will destroy entire countries. Bad shepherds will be removed from all walks of life: leaders in the church, government, public and private bosses, and bad parents. The list goes on.

Believe it or not, Jesus is coming. Everything listed above are signs of His second return to this earth. We are presently experiencing His warning voice, His patience and His Longsuffering in so many ways, saying, get ready 'Repent' and prepare to meet Jesus, the King of kings and Lord of lords! God is so loving, merciful and kind He is giving us enough time to make that final decision. He said, you have a chance to choose either eternal-life having sweet fellowship with the Trinity or eternal-death tormented with Satan. Jesus said, let me help you to choose because it is your final choice, beyond this choice there's no turning back, or reversing gear like that of a vehicle. God in His loving kindness finally said, 'Choose Life' and live eternally! He is a pardoning and a forgiving Saviour, if we refused to follow His loving choice pointing us into that right direction, then we have no one to blame but ourselves (our forefather Adam blamed Eve and Eve finally blamed the Serpent/Satan), therefore we are all without excuse!

Matthew 24.

1 And Jesus went out, and departed from the temple: and his disciples came to him for to shew him the buildings of the temple.

2 And Jesus said unto them, See ye not all these things? verily I say unto you, There shall not be left here one stone upon another, that shall not be thrown down.

3 And as he sat upon the mount of Olives, the disciples came unto him privately, saying, Tell us, when shall these things be? and what shall be the sign of thy coming, and of the end of the world?

4 And Jesus answered and said unto them, Take heed that no man deceive you.

5 For many shall come in my name, saying, I am Christ; and shall deceive many.

6 And ye shall hear of wars and rumours of wars: see that ye be not troubled: for all these things must come to pass, but the end is not yet.

7 For nation shall rise against nation, and kingdom against kingdom: and there shall be famines, and pestilences, and earthquakes, in divers' places.

8 All these are the beginning of sorrows.

9 Then shall they deliver you up to be afflicted, and shall kill you: and ye shall be hated of all nations for my name's sake.

10 And then shall many be offended, and shall betray one another, and shall hate one another.

11 And many false prophets shall rise, and shall deceive many.

12 And because iniquity shall abound, the love of many shall wax cold.

13 But he that shall endure unto the end, the same shall be saved.

14 And this gospel of the kingdom shall be preached in all the world for a witness unto all nations; and then shall the end come.

15 When ye therefore shall see the abomination of desolation, spoken of by Daniel the prophet, stand in the holy place, (whoso readeth, let him understand:)

16 Then let them which be in Judaea flee into the mountains:

17 Let him which is on the housetop not come down to take any thing out of his house:

18 Neither let him which is in the field return back to take his clothes.

19 And woe unto them that are with child, and to them that give suck in those days!

20 But pray ye that your flight be not in the winter, neither on the sabbath day:

21 For then shall be great tribulation, such as was not since the beginning of the world to this time, no, nor ever shall be.

22 And except those days should be shortened, there should no flesh be saved: but for the elect's sake those days shall be shortened.

23 Then if any man shall say unto you, Lo, here is Christ, or there; believe it not.

24 For there shall arise false Christs, and false prophets, and shall shew great signs and wonders; insomuch that, if it were possible, they shall deceive the very elect.

25 Behold, I have told you before.

26 Wherefore if they shall say unto you, Behold, he is in the desert; go not forth: behold, he is in the secret chambers; believe it not.

27 For as the lightning cometh out of the east, and shineth even unto the west; so shall also the coming of the Son of man be.

28 For wheresoever the carcase is, there will the eagles be gathered together.

29 Immediately after the tribulation of those days shall the sun be darkened, and the moon shall not give her light, and the stars shall fall from heaven, and the powers of the heavens shall be shaken:

30 And then shall appear the sign of the Son of man in heaven: and then shall all the tribes of the earth mourn, and they shall see the Son of man coming in the clouds of heaven with power and great glory.

31 And he shall send his angels with a great sound of a trumpet, and they shall gather together his elect from the four winds, from one end of heaven to the other.

32 Now learn a parable of the fig tree; When his branch is yet tender, and putteth forth leaves, ye know that summer is nigh:

33 So likewise ye, when ye shall see all these things, know that it is near, even at the doors.

34 Verily I say unto you, This generation shall not pass, till all these things be fulfilled.

35 Heaven and earth shall pass away, but my words shall not pass away.

36 But of that day and hour knoweth no man, no, not the angels of heaven, but my Father only.

37 But as the days of Noah were, so shall also the coming of the Son of man be.

38 For as in the days that were before the flood they were eating and drinking, marrying and giving in marriage, until the day that Noah entered into the ark,

39 And knew not until the flood came, and took them all away; so shall also the coming of the Son of man be.

40 Then shall two be in the field; the one shall be taken, and the other left.

41 Two women shall be grinding at the mill; the one shall be taken, and the other left.

42 Watch therefore: for ye know not what hour your Lord doth come.

43 But know this, that if the goodman of the house had known in what watch the thief would come, he would have watched, and would not have suffered his house to be broken up.

44 Therefore be ye also ready: for in such an hour as ye think not the Son of man cometh.

45 Who then is a faithful and wise servant, whom his lord hath made ruler over his household, to give them meat in due season?

46 Blessed is that servant, whom his lord when he cometh shall find so doing.

47 Verily I say unto you, That he shall make him ruler over all his goods.

48 But and if that evil servant shall say in his heart, My lord delayeth his coming;

49 And shall begin to smite his fellowservants, and to eat and drink with the drunken;

50 The lord of that servant shall come in a day when he looketh not for him, and in an hour that he is not aware of,

51 And shall cut him asunder, and appoint him his portion with the hypocrites: there shall be weeping and gnashing of teeth.

GAS MELTED THE FLESH OF HUMAN BEINGS.

I remembered giving my heart to God, making a profession of faith; I got saved at the age of 13years.This soldier, T C Taylor, a Jamaican, came to St. Kitts, preaching the Gospel, in May of 1967, during the course of him evangelizing; I gave my life to Jesus. Four years later, I got baptized in the Name of the Father, the Son, and the Holy Spirit; I was then seventeen years old.

This Evangelist was a big powerful man, with a thunderous voice. He said he was a "bad man" in those days, who served in the Jamaican Army for many years. He said, he heard the preaching of the Gospel message, the Word of God, the good news of Salvation. He said, normally he would never listen to any preaching whatsoever but this time he listened and it was the working of the Spirit of God, which he had no power to resist. People when God the Holy Spirit is striving with you it is hard to resist, it is the hand of God and the voice of God in operation. As strong as he knew he was, he was as weak as a little child that night, he humbled himself and gave his life and heart to God. He said, from that time it was a miracle for him all the way. This Jamaican Soldier is a typical example of the Apostle Paul whom God met on the road of Damascus. God struck him down taking away his physical sight, eventually the Holy Spirit of God sent him help, restoring his sight, setting him on the path of God's will, plan and purpose for his life.

Like the Apostle Paul, God called the former Jamaican Soldier, to preach the Gospel. God the Holy Spirit trained him making him an Evangelist touring all over the world, preaching the Gospel of Salvation, which is good news, telling us what Jesus Christ can do to reconcile sinners to God.

In Romans 1:16, the Apostle Paul said, "For I am not ashamed of the Gospel of Christ: for it is the power of God unto salvation to everyone that believeth; to the Jew first, and also to the Greek."

The preaching of the Gospel instructs us about a Holy, pure, perfect and righteous God; the God-head of the Trinity of God the Father, God the Son, God the Holy Spirit. This includes the wonderful work of His great creation of heaven, earth and all therein. It also tells us about the sweet fellowship between God and mankind in the Garden of Eden. In addition, it tells us about the fall of man, when he was deceived by the enemy Satan, causing him to sin and break fellowship with God. Fellowship between God and man came to an end because God cannot have fellowship with sin and darkness, because He is light, righteous and pure.

Although man has sinned, God still loves us and wants to continue sweet fellowship with man, therefore He sent His Son Jesus, His only begotten son, to die for us on the cross for our sins. Shedding His blood was the only solution to wash our sins away, restoring our fellowship with God.

Jesus died on the cross, shedding His blood. He was buried and rose from the grave, in great power, proving that He is alive. Later He ascended into heaven, seen by man. He said He has gone to prepare a place for all mankind, to live with Him forever; He will come again in the rapture for all who opened their hearts and accepted His salvation. Man would be reconciled with God once more.

John 3:16 (KJV) **reads,** "For God so loved the world that he gave his only begotten Son, that whosoever believeth in him should not perish, but have everlasting life."

For many years I knew God the Holy Spirit was operating in my life, but did not understand it for many years because many churches lacked the five-fold ministry in those days. Church leaders did their best, but there was still a need for the action of these spiritual gifts among believers.

I will reveal to you at this time, this dream that God the Holy Spirit gave to me during my mid-teens. I remember the dream as if it was yesterday. I have never revealed this dream to anyone. It was approximately forty-four years ago.

I was between sixteen and eighteen years of age, the dream was about the smelling of Gas which melted the flesh of man while walking.

In this dream, it was day and I was walking the streets doing what I had to do, then without any warning, I started smelling gas. It was a strange smell. I was walking within the area where our Island's gas is stored; therefore, I thought it was the usual scent one would experience within that area. The scent became stronger and I became concerned.

I was accustomed to smell different types of gases, but this scent was different. As I walked, it seemed as though I was walking towards the smell. I quickly covered my nose and before I could say or do anything, I looked at the people around, they were walking about and their flesh was just melting from their bodies. Everyone started to run but it seemed that running was in vain, the deadly gas had already polluted the entire atmosphere unknown to everyone. I woke up shortly after having that dream.

Today is Thursday, August 20th, 2015, and I am writing this long forgotten dream, which God the Holy Spirit brought to my attention to share with the rest of the world. God is in control and He is speaking to us in numerous ways of which this is one.

People let us take heed and respond to the voice of God the Holy Spirit as He speaks so loud and clear. This is another warning from God He is saying to us, get ready and be prepared because His coming is very near. There is no way of escaping the awful wrath of God, there is no place for man to run and hide. For God to bring this dream to my remembrance 44–45 years later is indeed a valid reason to seek Him. Are we going to experience a surprise Nuclear-Gas-Attack on mankind Although these things are taking place right before our very eyes yet, more than half of the world's population is unmoved, mentally asleep, and unconcerned with no intention of adjusting their lives. This is the trickery of Satan, using deception, blinding the eyes of mankind, saying, do not worry, there is still time available to you! Deception! The Bible reminds us, as it was in the days of Noah, so shall it be in the coming of the Son of man (Jesus). In the time of Noah, the people, hardened their hearts, stiffened their necks and refused to believe that they were going through climate change, each day it became worse.

REVELATION . . . THE REMOVAL OF "BAD SHEPHERDS" FROM THE EARTH.

God the ONLY CREATOR. He created us and blessed us with the image of Himself, proving His unconditional love to us and for us. It matters not of our, colour (red, green, yellow, pink or cream), language, nationality, religion, society or creed. We had the most precious and perfect privilege of having sweet fellowship with God and this cause great jealously in the heart of Satan. Satan hates the atmosphere of the bond of love, peace and unity, which enriched our sweet fellowship with God and decided to put an end to it. Then since he is the 'Father of Lies' he used his plans of trickery and lies deceiving our 'fore parents' Adam and Eve, succeeded in breaking their sweet fellowship with God, sending them on the run trying to hide from God. Who told them that they have done wrong? God in creating mankind, wisely blessed us with a 'conscience,' which is alive, sharp and well, this always instantly tells us the perfect results of our actions, whether they are good or bad, before anyone else can past any judgment.

God is the 'Creator' of everything included Satan who wanted to be as powerful and as wise as God, but he has failed miserably failing to achieve his goal! God who is; light, love, pure and perfect could not continue to have sweet fellowship with man because He cannot fellowship with sin, unrighteousness and darkness. Therefore He gave us, the gift of His only Son, 'Jesus' who is; the way, the truth, the light and life eternal. Jesus voluntarily died, in our room on the cross, paying the price/debt for our sins because we were unworthy and unable to pay the price of our sins. Jesus death on the cross, shedding His precious blood, the only thing that is powerful enough to cleanse man from his sins. The blood of Jesus is so powerful, it is the only thing powerful enough to help us reinstating our sweet fellowship with God forevermore, but we still will have to acknowledge our sinfulness, repents, seeks His pardon and forgiveness then allows Him to wash us in the 'Blood of the Lamb.'

Jesus said, in John 10:11–14, reads, 'I am the good shepherd: the good shepherd giveth his life for the sheep. 12. But he that is and hireling, and not the shepherd, whose own the sheep are not, seeth the wolf coming, and leaveth the sheep, and fleeth: and the wolf catcheth them and scattereth the sheep. 13. The hireling fleeth because he is an hireling, and careth not for the sheep. 14. I am the good shepherd and know my sheep, and am known of mine.' Jesus is 'the Good Shepherd' and Satan is the wolf, hireling, and the bad shepherd, who still uses his trickery deceiving mankind today.

God who is in controls of everything, including the climate change, has seen the operation of man, the lack and absent of love and unity, still been deceived by Satan the bad shepherd. Deception started in the Garden of Eden, when man choose to listen to the voice of Satan, disobeying God's command. God has given us the power in making our own choice, although He said, 'Choose Life'! Why mankind are fighting for living long life on this earth but fighting against God's offers plan of salvation of living eternally, having sweet fellowship with, The Trinity of God the Father, God the Son, and God the Holy Spirit? Satan is working overtime using deception and everything in his power distracting man from listening to God and worshipping Him as Adam and Eve did before the deception of Satan. Sad to say, man is still listening to the voice and trickery of Satan deceiving themselves from obeying the voice of God the Holy Spirit.

In the Book of Joel: 2 vs 28—31, reads, 'And it shall come to pass afterwards, that I will pour out my spirit upon all flesh; and your sons and your daughters shall prophecy, your old men shall dream dreams, your young men shall see visions: And also upon the servants and upon the handmaids in those days will I pour out my spirit,

And I will show wonders in the heavens and in the earth, blood and fire, and pillows of smoke, The sun shall be turned into darkness, and the moon into blood, before the great and the terrible day of the Lord come. And it shall come to pass, that whosoever shall call on the name of the Lord shall be delivered: for in Mount Zion and in Jerusalem shall be deliverance, as the Lord hath said, and in the remnant whom the Lord shall call.'

Then in the Book of Acts: 2 vs 16 -21, reads, 'But, this is that which was spoken by the prophet Joel; and it shall come to pass in the last days, saith God, I will pour out of my Spirit upon all flesh: and your sons and daughters shall prophecy, and your young men shall see vision, and your old men shall dream dreams; and on my servants and on my handmaids I will pour out in those days of my Spirit; and they shall prophecy: and I will show wonders in heaven above, and signs in the earth beneath; blood, and fire, and vapour of smoke: the sun shall be turned into darkness, and the moon into blood, before that great and notable day of the Lord come: and it shall come to pass, that whosoever shall call upon the name of the Lord shall be save.'

People, from the moment Satan started his deception in the beginning in the Garden of Eden deceiving our fore-parents Adam and Eve, he never stop or takes a holiday but with great determinations fulfilling his heart's desires of, the total deception of mankind! Are we going to be double determined when faces with his temptations and tricks of deceptions? Today mankind are being tricked and deceived by Satan in ways most people would never expect, such as using your best-loved-trusted friend whom you always boasting about putting your entire-life on the Line/Edge for . . . both mentally and physically lays down and die without fighting back because of the bond of love, unity and 110% trust in our friends (Judas the deceiver)! The spirit of Judas is alive and actively operating in every areas of life that involves mankind.

Today, a large percentage of earth's populations are deceived and continues to be deceived by the trickery of Satan. Just think of the millions of prisons throughout the entire world, overflowing with men and women of all ages, deceived by the subtle, trickery of Satan . . . all saying 'If and but' when it is always too late!

In this Revelation, God said, I am going to remove from the earth those 'IBad Shepherds' from the; churches, governments, businesses, society including parents! People, I received this Revelation in a dream from God, on the 12th October, 2011, I shared this dream with many people, and also I can remember sharing it with the congregation one night, at the church which I attended. Also, I vividly remember that on the eighth day of receiving this dream, the Libyan leader died! When this world known leader died on the 20/10/2011, it was the beginning of the Revelation of this dream and I can remember making note of this mile stone of what God the Holy Spirit said to me. From that day Libya leader died, I can remember many more world leaders too died and since that memorial incident many more leaders who fits the role as 'Bad Shepherds' also died and this is an ongoing process until this very day. I can vividly records the death and removal of many leaders included in these removals were many parents. People when God speaks it is a warning to all mankind, then action always take its course because God word is true, He cannot lie and His promises never fails because He always fulfils His spoken 'Word'! In a written letter of the Apostle Paul, to Titus, his son in the Faith, in the first chapter and verse two (2), this is what the Apostle Paul written as he described God to Titus. It reads, 'In hope of eternal life, which God, that cannot lie, promised before the world began.'

God is unhappy with man and his choice of still listening and been deceived by Satan. PEOPLE, just look around and you can see countless evidence of the deception of Satan in dealing with mankind. We can find examples in all areas of life; in our own life, children, parents, homes, schools, colleges, universities, work-place, sports, churches, politics, religions and the long list continues. Satan want mankind to live a life of deception until death when it is too late . . . to the point where there is no turning back! Satan has succeeded by having deceived multitudes of millions of people and sad to say, **'TODAY, THEY ARE ALL IN HELL AWAITING GOD'S FURY AND WRATH WHICH WILL BE POURED OUT ON SATAN AND ALL WHO ARE DECEIVED BY HIM . . . AMONG THEM AWAITING ARE MILLIONS OF SPIRITUAL LEADERS; PASTORS, BISHOPS, EVANGELISTS, FAITH-HEALERS, MINISTERS, REVERANDS, WORLD KNOWN ELEQUANT**

SPEAKERS, PRIESTS, WORLD-LEADERS, GOVERNMENT-LEADERS, LEADERS IN SOCIETY, BAD-PARENTS AND ALL THOSE BAD SHEPHERDS AND WOLF'S WHO LED THE FLOCK OF SHEEP ASTRAY GONE AND GOING TO HELL WITH THEM'! SAD! SAD! O HOW SAD TO SEE THE LENGTH AND BREATH SATAN WENT BLINDING THE EYES OF MANKIND LEADING THEM INTO HIS TRAP, DECEIVING THEM UNTIL DEATH . . . TOO LATE IS NOW THEIR CRIES!

People, God the Holy Spirit has open up my spiritual eyes and has shown me the condition of man, having their physical eyes wide open but mentally blind-folded going to hell deceived by Satan. God the Holy Spirit said, 'Satan is using DESEPTION deceiving the world taking them to hell with him, the place which is prepared for Satan and the fallen angels, a place where the fire never quenched, the worms lives on forever tormenting; Satan, the fallen-angels and mankind. In this place there are weeping, screaming, anguish and languishing cries of eternal-pain. Today God the Holy Spirit send me with this message to you (The Entire World), warning you to flee the awful wrath of God the place of torment (HELL)! Many people are allowing Satan to say to them . . . there is no HELL! People, please do not be deceived, there is a God and there is a Satan, there is a Hell and there is a Heaven (the place where Jesus lives)! As a reminder, remember the people in Noah's days, they were people like us today . . . ignorant, having their own ways, living it up, having fun, and they were deceived by Satan. People please do not do like those people in Noah's days! Noah preached for 120 years, warning the people, they called him crazy, they did not believe that it was a message from God to them. He continues until the Lord say, 'Noah, it is time, come into the Ark and let me shut the door,' then God finally shut the door! Then it was only when the rain begins to fall, then it was at that point the people start to believe the MESSAGE and the messenger of God! It was then too late, because God already shut the door and not even Noah had the power to open the door! Those people then realized they were deceived by Satan but it was too late! Sad to say, these people, they perished in the flood and are in hell waiting their final verdict from God our 'Creator'! People please believe the message, do not be deceived by the tricks of Satan . . . believe the message, repent, invite the Lord Jesus into your hearts, allows Him to save you and wash you in His precious Blood, live for him and be sure of eternal life when he comes or if you dies before He comes. People this can be God's final call to you! Would you open your heart's door and let Him in? The Saviour of the world, Jesus the one who died for all mankind!

Let Him In 'Jesus'!

He waits outside your Heart's Door,
Let Him in 'Jesus,' before He departs,
TODAY can be His Last visit,
To return 'No More.'
He 'Loves you!
He is 'The only Way, the Truth and Life Eternal'!
He died to save you!
He wants to Abide in your Heart,
He wants to give you Eternal Life,
Would you open your Heart's Door?
He's waiting for you to make your Choice,
Between Life and Death, Jesus said, 'Choose Life'!
As He gently knocks, let Him in, 'Jesus'!
Let the Saviour in!
Author John A Hodge.

God is Perfect, Holy, Pure, and Righteous and just, and although He loves us 'Unconditionally' He is a hater of sin, darkness and unrighteousness, therefore no one with sin in their lives cannot enter God's righteous heaven. If a man dies in his sins he will go to hell, please do not believes these lies these preachers telling you. These people are workers of Satan deceiving people, hiding behind a name (pastor, priest, minister etc.). If one commits suicide, this is the deception of Satan and he or she has made their choice, choosing Hell and eternal punishment, which is the wrath of God's judgment! If one died in an accident, plane crash, or someone killed them or died naturally, 'Without Repenting' and meeting God's plan of salvation, they are going to hell! Over the years these 'Spiritual Leaders' have been telling you lies and watering down things, hiding the truth from you . . . some will say mostly at funerals, 'well, we shall rise from the graves one day, yes, but what they hides from telling you is that, there are going to be 'Two Resurrections,' one for those who died in Christ (those who repents of their sins) and then one for those who died in their sins! People often say, 'when they died that's it, it is all over, that's the end! Oh No! This is the total deception of Satan, after death there is a judgment-day awaiting all men to answer to God for their life on this earth and it is called God's Judgment-day! At this day, some will hear these words, 'depart from me I do not know you'! Then naturally you will be cast into the, lake of fire, the pit of hell, with Satan and the fallen angels. People do not be ignorant, avoid the deception of Satan! Some of these 'Wolf's in sheep clothing, preaches from their pulpits, saying, 'Born again is not important'! This again in a Lie from the pit of hell deceiving you! In this Gospel of John, Jesus said, if any man want to go to heaven, that person 'Must Be Born Again'! Later in verse seven (7), Nicodemus this rich ruler, too like some of these stubborn and ignorant preachers try to argue with Jesus, on the topic of 'Born Again.' Then Jesus said to Nicodemus, do not argue with me Mr. Man, ' Marvel not that I said unto thee, Ye must be born again'! Today all those preachers, who preached, teaches and died without been 'Born Again,' are today in hell awaiting the wrath of God on them! These spiritual-leaders (Bad Shepherds), were all deceived by the tricks of Satan! Sad to say, 'Oh how foolish'!

John 3 King James Version.
3 There was a man of the Pharisees, named Nicodemus, a ruler of the Jews:
2 The same came to Jesus by night, and said unto him, Rabbi, we know that thou art a teacher come from God: for no man can do these miracles that thou doest, except God be with him.
3 Jesus answered and said unto him, Verily, verily, I say unto thee, Except a man be born again, he cannot see the kingdom of God.
4 Nicodemus saith unto him, How can a man be born when he is old? can he enter the second time into his mother's womb, and be born?

[5] Jesus answered, Verily, verily, I say unto thee, Except a man be born of water and of the Spirit, he cannot enter into the kingdom of God.
[6] That which is born of the flesh is flesh; and that which is born of the Spirit is spirit.
[7] Marvel not that I said unto thee, Ye must be born again.
[8] The wind bloweth where it listeth, and thou hearest the sound thereof, but canst not tell whence it cometh, and whither it goeth: so is every one that is born of the Spirit.
[9] Nicodemus answered and said unto him, How can these things be?
[10] Jesus answered and said unto him, Art thou a master of Israel, and knowest not these things?
[11] Verily, verily, I say unto thee, We speak that we do know, and testify that we have seen; and ye receive not our witness.
[12] If I have told you earthly things, and ye believe not, how shall ye believe, if I tell you of heavenly things?
[13] And no man hath ascended up to heaven, but he that came down from heaven, even the Son of man which is in heaven.
[14] And as Moses lifted up the serpent in the wilderness, even so must the Son of man be lifted up:
[15] That whosoever believeth in him should not perish, but have eternal life.
[16] For God so loved the world, that he gave his only begotten Son, that whosoever believeth in him should not perish, but have everlasting life.
[17] For God sent not his Son into the world to condemn the world; but that the world through him might be saved.
[18] He that believeth on him is not condemned: but he that believeth not is condemned already, because he hath not believed in the name of the only begotten Son of God.
[19] And this is the condemnation, that light is come into the world, and men loved darkness rather than light, because their deeds were evil.
[20] For every one that doeth evil hateth the light, neither cometh to the light, lest his deeds should be reproved.
[21] But he that doeth truth cometh to the light, that his deeds may be made manifest, that they are wrought in God.
[22] After these things came Jesus and his disciples into the land of Judaea; and there he tarried with them, and baptized.

²³ And John also was baptizing in Aenon near to Salim, because there was much water there: and they came, and were baptized.

²⁴ For John was not yet cast into prison.

²⁵ Then there arose a question between some of John's disciples and the Jews about purifying.

²⁶ And they came unto John, and said unto him, Rabbi, he that was with thee beyond Jordan, to whom thou barest witness, behold, the same baptizeth, and all men come to him.

²⁷ John answered and said, A man can receive nothing, except it be given him from heaven.

²⁸ Ye yourselves bear me witness, that I said, I am not the Christ, but that I am sent before him.

²⁹ He that hath the bride is the bridegroom: but the friend of the bridegroom, which standeth and heareth him, rejoiceth greatly because of the bridegroom's voice: this my joy therefore is fulfilled.

³⁰ He must increase, but I must decrease.

³¹ He that cometh from above is above all: he that is of the earth is earthly, and speaketh of the earth: he that cometh from heaven is above all.

³² And what he hath seen and heard, that he testifieth; and no man receiveth his testimony.

³³ He that hath received his testimony hath set to his seal that God is true.

³⁴ For he whom God hath sent speaketh the words of God: for God giveth not the Spirit by measure unto him.

³⁵ The Father loveth the Son, and hath given all things into his hand.

³⁶ He that believeth on the Son hath everlasting life: and he that believeth not the Son shall not see life; but the wrath of God abideth on him.

People, all those spiritual-leaders standing on or behind the pulpit preaching the word of God, most of them are not called by God! No! First in order to be called by God serving and working for Him you cannot serve no other master but God and God alone! A lot of those who are called spiritual leaders standing behind the pulpit, leading the congregation, and are still members of all these societies . . . God do not know them and they do not know God. God cannot fellowship with darkness, because you cannot serve two masters at the same time, you must make a choice, either God or your old master! So if you are still members of your societies, serving your old master, you cannot be working for God! Therefore these are the ones Satan are using to deceive the people in the churches all over this world. They are not real, they are wolves in sheep clothing or 'Bad Shepherds.' These are some of the 'Bad Shepherds,' God the Holy Spirit speaks of removing from the earth.

People, all these Pastors, Preachers, Ministers, Evangelists, Reverends, Bishops, Prophets, Faith-healer, and Apostles . . . some are called and send by God others were neither called or send by God.

Some of these people standing behind the pulpits are called by God to shepherd the flock of sheep entrusted in their care. It is said if anyone have intention of making big and quick bucks/money, you can choose from two jobs . . . either open a church or be a politician! And this is one of the criteria cause many to be standing behind your pulpits and are called your pastors. Therefore a large percentages of those standing behind the pulpits today are not saved and do not have any intimacy with God.

Others are behind the pulpit because of these reasons;
1) Some went to college did theology and trained as a minister.
2) An advert saying, church seeking Full Time Pastor . . . a job.
3) Others were chosen by the church committee.
4) Few grew up in the church, went through the Sunday school and a member.
5) Traditionally, a family hand-me-down position.
6) Another chosen, charismatically having the gift of an eloquent speaker.
7) Another group chosen because they had a good knowledge of the word.
8) Some came to an agreement; people are calling him Pastor, he preaches like a Pastor and have the looks of a Pastor, so let us make him our Pastor . . . and the list goes on.

In order to be working for God one must have one main qualification and this main or major qualification is 'LOVE'! Without the qualification of 'LOVE,' no one can work for God! First God is 'LOVE' and 'LOVE' is God!

The Apostle Paul, written in 1 Corinthians: 13, stating the main qualification all needs to major in in order to be truly committed in serving and working for God is 'LOVE.'

1 Corinthians: 13 . . . Charity means LOVE.

Though I speak with the tongues of men and of angels, and have not charity, I am become as sounding brass, or a tinkling cymbal. 2And though I have the gift of prophecy, and understand all mysteries, and all knowledge; and though I have all faith, so that I could remove mountains, and have not charity, I am nothing. 3And though I bestow all my goods to feed the poor, and though I give my body to be burned, and have not charity, it profiteth me nothing.

4 Charity suffereth long, and is kind; charity envieth not; charity vaunteth not itself, is not puffed up, 5 Doth not behave itself unseemly, seeketh not her own, is not easily provoked, thinketh no evil; 6 Rejoiceth not in iniquity, but rejoiceth in the truth; 7Beareth all things, believeth all things, hopeth all things, endureth all things.

8 Charity never faileth: but whether there be prophecies, they shall fail; whether there be tongues, they shall cease; whether there be knowledge, it shall vanish away. 9 For we know in part, and we prophesy in part. 10 But when that which is perfect is come, then that which is in part shall be done away.11 When I was a child, I spake as a child, I understood as a child, I thought as a child: but when I became a man, I put away childish things. 12For now we see through a glass, darkly; but then face to face: now I know in part; but then shall I know even as also I am known. 13 And now abideth faith, hope, charity, these three; but the greatest of these is charity (LOVE).

The Apostle Peter is a good example of a 'Good Shepherd,' displaying and demonstrating his 'LOVE 'for the flock of sheep entrusted in his care. Peter was a well-known popular fisherman, who was totally dedicated and committed loving his work/trade. Then one day his entire life changed almost instantly, taking, not only a U-turn but a 360 degree spun when he came in contact with Jesus, who called him and said, follow me and I will make you fishers of men! Jesus saw how much Peter loved his work of fishing and his dedication to it, so in calling him, Jesus wanted him to transferees all his love and dedication into working for Him as a Disciple. Later Peter during the training processed by Jesus getting himself formula with his new task, his mind wondered back and wanted to do the two jobs at the same time because he felt there was a missing link because he missed both the trade and the money he was making. Jesus saw it and confronted Peter on the topic of surrendering his total 'LOVE' to the work of which he was called to do. (Hymn 'Channel only').

Jesus confronted Peter concerning his love for the work for which he was called to do. Jesus is indeed the 'Good Shepherd,' called Peter, training and making him the first ever earthly 'Shepherd' to tend for the flock of sheep that is placed in him care. Peter and some of the disciples went fishing, then after toiling and caught nothing, Jesus in the distant instructed them where to cast their nets, and to their surprised their catch were so great they had to be aided by another boat to bring the so many fish ashore. Then after reaching ashore, they made a fire and prepared some to eat. Jesus also were present, He blessed the supper and after dining, Jesus said unto Peter, "So when they had dined, Jesus saith to Simon Peter, Simon, son of Jonas, lovest thou me more than these? He saith unto him, Yea, Lord; thou knowest that I love thee. He saith unto him, Feed my lambs. [16] He saith to him again the second time, Simon, son of Jonas, lovest thou me? He saith unto him, Yea, Lord; thou knowest that I love thee. He saith unto him, Feed my sheep. [17] He saith unto him the third time, Simon, son of Jonas, lovest thou me? Peter was grieved because he said unto him the third time, Lovest thou me? And he said unto him, Lord, thou knowest all things; thou knowest that I love thee. Jesus saith unto him, Feed my sheep" (John 21:15–17).

Jesus gave Peter an exam on the topic of 'LOVE' preparing and training him for the task and duty of a Good Shepherd. After dining, Jesus said unto Peter, 'Peter, do you love me more than these fish? Peter replied, 'Yes, Lord; 'you knows I love you'! Jesus said unto him, 'feed my lambs! Jesus almost in the same breath, repeated the same question to Peter and Peter replied the same as he did in the first question. Then Jesus said unto him, 'feed my sheep'! Jesus for the third time repeated himself on the topic of 'LOVE,' Peter got real astonished, concerned and was grieved in his heart because this is the third time Jesus questioning him on the topic of his, 'LOVE, for Him and his love for the fish. Peter replied in tears, saying, 'Lord you who knows everything included my heart, you knows I really and truly 'LOVE' you! Peter were aware that Jesus knew our heart's desires therefore we cannot deceived him by lying to Him. First Jesus said to Peter, feed my 'LAMBS' because they were new, young and tender . . . all new born Christians are babies in God's sight they are 'Tender Lambs,' this have nothing to do with age, therefore much tender loving care in very imperative in this case. Then secondly Jesus said to him, if you truly love me more that the fish, then feed my 'SHEEP,' Jesus is now saying to Peter they have grown both physically and spiritually, therefore tender loving care is still important . . . as a Shepherd you must be knowledgeable of the kind of solid food that is needed at this stage of their growth. Then for the third and final time Jesus said to Peter, 'If you really 'LOVE' me more that these fish, then your full-time-job is to be a 'Good Shepherd,' to this flock of sheep; loving, feeding and caring for them at all times . . . in other words, this is now your total, committed full-time-job! And remember to guard yourself from the distractions, trickery and deception of Satan additional side-line job offering of business and partnerships. All these side-line job offers are distractions and destructions to your 'LOVE' as a 'Good Shepherd,' to the flock entrusted in your care!

Jesus, is saying to Peter, I am the 'Good Shepherd,' so I am training you to be a 'Good Shepherd,' just like me. As a Shepherd, caring for the flock of sheep, 'LOVE' is very important because patience is greatly needed at all times looking after the flock of sheep. Jesus was saying to Peter you're 'LOVE' as a Shepherd must be committed, steadfast, genuine and dying 'LOVE' for the flock of sheep. Jesus, was saying to Peter, you must love them with all your heart, remember they are all in your care, needs to grow stronger day by day to the point of full maturity taking on great responsibilities. This will aids you in expanding, planting more churches and continue training others to be 'Good Shepherds' caring for new flock of sheep without having to be deceived by Satan the father of lies! People take warning, this is no fairy-tail or bed time story but everything is reality. Avoid the deception of Satan, again just look around and see the havoc he is doing to so many of our; children, homes, families, parents, friends, bosses, sporting-arenas, world-leaders, government-leaders, spiritual-leaders, society and everyone. Satan is buying, laughing and playing for time! Please, avoid the pit-fall of hell, the awful wrath and punishment of God! God loves you and all He wants is for you to repents and accepts Him as your Saviour . . . All He wants is to continue living forever having 'Sweet Fellowship' with man eternally.

People because we are living in the last and closing days, Satan is nervous, he knows his time of punishment is drawing neigh so he is busy using deception looking for as many people as possible to joins and shares in his punishment of torment in the lake of fire in hell! Satan hates to see mankind living in unity, harmony and love among themselves, so he is using his best weapon of deception, remember Jesus kept on repeating to mankind to be strong and beware of 'Deception' in every areas of life. Every moment of every day we are, seeing, reading and hearing news of deception making headline every day in almost every literature we can pick up to read, such as;

> Satan, took a swing at the world football body of sports 'Fifa.' Satan in this case he went back over two thousand years ago when Jesus was crucified, using his deception. Satan dangled money deceiving Judas, who sold Jesus for thirty (30) pieces of silver, then when it was all done, Satan finally laughed at him (Judas) and caused him to hang himself! The spirit of Judas is yet still alive operating and destroying millions of lives. All this is the tricks of Satan, trying to destroying this world football sporting organisation using his tricks of deception of the 'Tongue,' destroying; decades of sweet-friendship and happy-relationship. People it matters not who get this role/job, none will do as much as Mr. S. Blatter . . . he reached out and helped poor and needy undeveloped countries, making young sport lovers happy, giving them an opportunity fulfilling their desires and dreams of making football a reality comes true! No one is perfect! Oh no! But yes, I do condemns wrong doings! Mr. S. Blatter will one day be looked upon as a 'Saint,' when compared with all who succeeded

him! There's a popular phrase often quotes by many people world-wide, which is so true, 'do not cry/ball for who is leaving but cry/ball for who is coming and in most cases this phrase has proven to be true! Can you and I see the 'Hearts' of those who seeks this job? No! Everyone who seeks this job has their own agendas, which they will never speaks of! I believe that Mr. S. Blatter has a heart of love for the sport but most of all a 'Vision,' for the present and future generation football lovers, especially those living in undeveloped, poor and needy countries! My Bible tells me in Psalm: 41, it speaks of those who helps the 'Poor and Needy.' In the first verse it clearly said, 'BLESSED is he that considered the poor and needy'! Mr. S. Blatter, the word of the Lord said, you are 'Blessed' and the Lord God Himself will reward you for fulfilling this command! Satan hates helping the poor and needy folks. Look at those who are fleeing for their lives . . . God said, help them and receives great blessings from Him! In every organisation there are 'Judas,' whom Satan uses to carry out him work of deception. Mr. S. Blatter, as human we find it hard to forgive those who have done us wrong, but Jesus said, we have to first forgive those who have done us wrong in order for Him to forgive us of our wrong-doings (sins). There's no neutral grounds in this important matter of truth and righteousness seeking God's face and having fellowship with Him . . . remember God who is light cannot fellowship with unrighteousness and darkness. I encourages you to give your heart to the Lord and experienced richly the fulfilment of His word, to you, your family and your future generations . . . this is the word of the Lord! You are blessed! Sir, on behalf of all those who were greatly blessed by your heart of 'Love' I now say a big 'Thank You and God's forever blessings'! People let us ask the Lord to help us to control our 'Tongue.' Satan delights in deceiving us when we uses our 'Tongue' negatively.

Psalm 41 King James Version.

41 Blessed is he that considereth the poor: the Lord will deliver him in time of trouble.

[2] The Lord will preserve him, and keep him alive; and he shall be blessed upon the earth: and thou wilt not deliver him unto the will of his enemies.

[3] The Lord will strengthen him upon the bed of languishing: thou wilt make all his bed in his sickness.

[4] I said, Lord, be merciful unto me: heal my soul; for I have sinned against thee.

[5] Mine enemies speak evil of me, When shall he die, and his name perish?

[6] And if he come to see me, he speaketh vanity: his heart gathereth iniquity to itself; when he goeth abroad, he telleth it.

[7] All that hate me whisper together against me: against me do they devise my hurt.

[8] An evil disease, say they, cleaveth fast unto him: and now that he lieth he shall rise up no more.

[9] Yea, mine own familiar friend, in whom I trusted, which did eat of my bread, hath lifted up his heel against me.

[10] But thou, O Lord, be merciful unto me, and raise me up, that I may requite them.

[11] By this I know that thou favourest me, because mine enemy doth not triumph over me.

[12] And as for me, thou upholdest me in mine integrity, and settest me before thy face for ever.

[13] Blessed be the Lord God of Israel from everlasting, and to everlasting. Amen, and Amen.

The Improper use of Our 'Tongue.' Can we Control Our 'Tongue'?

The 'Tongue,' is a Dangerous Weapon.
And an Uncontrolled Missile.

The 'Tongue,' is small yet can create Grave consequences,
The 'Tongue,' is the source of Numerous untold evils.

It Lifts up man, placing him on the mountaintop then puts him deep down in the valley below,
It Praises and brings total Destructions,
It splits forever; sweet loving families, trustworthy friends, and second to none relationships.
Energetically; it brags always, lies without warning, flatters for fun, gossips for recreation, and complains even while sleeping,
Tirelessly; it continues to curse nonstop, manipulates forever, and belittles without fear
And dynamically, deceitfully and delightfully an Urgent Agent of False-Hood.
It is a Fire, its dangerous red hot flames of jealousy,
Reminds us of Cain, who slew his brother Abel!
And finally sweeps and destroys everything in its path.
It is an awaiting time-bomb, ready to explore.
God who is Love, His Holy Spirit, can control our 'Tongue,'
By Operating on our Hearts and Minds,

Let Him forever control our Lives!

Author John A. Hodge.

SATAN BOLDLY ATTEMPTED TO DECEIVE JESUS.

P eople whether you want to believe it or not, the moment birth was given to us we were under attack and at war with Satan, whose aims and desperate desire is to destroy man totally using his main trick of 'Deception.' Just a reminder, Satan dislikes unity and oneness among mankind having a good-time in fellowship among themselves and with God our creator. He is unhappy to see sweet harmony; individually, as a loving couple, friends togetherness, family rich bonding, societal uniqueness of understanding, sports teamwork, political agreement, government positive movements, church growth, Christian faithfulness to God, youth courage, as well as the strength of islands, countries, nations, and world populations bonded by love. Satan is always at war with; himself, the fallen angels like him and man because we are forever loved, blessed and given power by God and finally because he wanted to be equally powerful as God, ruling His Kingdom as the King of kings and Lord of lords.

In the Gospel of Luke chapter 4, vs 1–15, we have a picture of Satan, bravely stepping up and challenging Jesus with his tricks of deception. Imagine the idiocy of Satan taking on the Son of God using temptation trying to deceive Jesus. People will ask this question: if Satan challenge Jesus the Perfect, Pure, Righteous, Just, and Holy One, then who am I as a man to overcome his deception? In this passage of scripture Jesus by demonstration practically showed us, how and what we need to do to overcome Satan's temptations and his tricks of deception. First we have to be daily studying the Word of God, memorizing it storing it in our hearts and finally quoting it and using it as a weapon against Satan, overcoming all his attacks of temptations and deceptions. People in this passage we are going to learn and see the power of the Word of God and the results thereof. Also we are going to see the delights of Satan, studying the Word of God, memorizing it, storing it in his heart and tried to use it as a weapon against Jesus in his tricks trying to deceive Him . . . but failed! Satan uses everything possible as hindrances and stumbling blocks hindering man from studying the Word of God but he is studying and memorising it because he knows the power of it and he is afraid of it. This is the reason he is using his trick of deception, hindering man from 'Memorizing' it (Word of God).

In the life of every Christian, one needs to set aside special times to seek God's face in areas of prayer and fasting, praise and worship, giving of tithes and offering, studying the Word of God, meditating and memorizing it, and, finally, a quiet time of silent listening to hear from Him with great expectation. Then, during this quiet time period of waiting and listening to hear from God, Satan usually appears showing up with his tricks of deceptions; therefore, man must be on guard and always prepared with the Word of God ready to use as missile against Satan.

Jesus were having a time of prayer and fasting as He emptied Himself physically, listening to hear from God the Father, for a spiritual refilling. The scripture said, Jesus was full of the Holy Ghost and was led by the Spirit into the wilderness. Jesus were fasting for forty days and forty nights and after such time he was physically hungry. Jesus was led by the Spirit into the wilderness, therefore He was under the control, direction and protection of God the Father. Satan knew He were hungry and in great need of food and water satisfying His physical needs . . . then used the opportunity trying to deceived him with his tricks. Satan knows the needs of man and always uses these opportunities to deceive mankind. Some people (none matured Christians) will respond, saying 'This is God' fulfilling our needs! This is the reason John said, as Christians we needs to try the Spirit to see whether they are of God, because we need to know our 'Shepherd's' voice as sheep of His flock. If a sheep do not know it's 'Shepherd's' voice, it is dangerously lost, easy prey to wolves and false shepherds.

Satan approached Jesus and said unto Him, I know you are hungry in needs of food, therefore if you are truly the Son of God, turn this stone into bread and satisfy you need! Jesus knew it was the deception of Satan, trying to trick Him by turning the stone into bread, obeying his (Satan) command and disobeying His Heavenly Father. Jesus then quoted the scripture, the Word of God the weapon Satan fears so much, 'And Jesus answered him, saying, It is written, That man shall not live by bread alone, but by every word of God.' Satan turned and went away, by the power of the quoted 'Word,' with determination to returns.

Jesus was led by the Spirit of God and did not allowed fear to control His way of living. Jesus, refused all invitation of dialog with Satan, all he did, was just quoted the powerful 'Word of God.' Satan came back for a second time refusing to give up. Satan took Him into a high mountain and showed Him the kingdom of the world at a glimpse and said unto him, all this is mine and the power thereof. I can give it to you, all you need to do is simple, Satan said, 'Worship me' and all is thine! How can Satan give Jesus all what is already belonging to His Heavenly Father? John remind us that all that the Father have is His! Jesus refused having any dialog with Satan, 'And Jesus answered and said unto him, Get thee behind me, Satan: for it is written, Thou shalt worship the Lord thy God, and him only shalt thou serve.'

In the wilderness, the children of Israel were tried and tested by Satan on endless occasion deceiving them, having them going around in circles because of disobedient to Moses and worshipping strange gods and idols all because of the deception of Satan. Without the leading of God the Holy Spirit, all our wilderness journeys are in jeopardy/trouble.

Jesus continued to depend on the leading and directions of His Heavenly Father doing His will. Satan never gives up, he kept on doing his best at all times to deceive men of all ages, he have no respect for positions or prestige, all his interest is the fulfilment of his deception. Satan for the third time, trying to deceive Jesus, took Him to the top of the pinnacle of a temple . . . the highest point. Satan choose to use the quoted Word of God to convinced Jesus, He (Jesus) will be safe because it is the 'Word of God.' Satan said unto Him, 'If thou be the Son of God, cast thyself down from hence: Satan knows Jesus is the Son of God.' Here Satan is persistent with his deceptions he never gives up. Satan quoted the 'Word of God,' again trying to deceive Jesus for the third time, but in this quote verse, Satan eliminated a very important part of the scripture trying to deceive Jesus. This is how Satan quoted this scripture saying, 'For it is written, He shall give his angels charge over thee, to keep thee': Satan took out the words, 'In all thy ways.' And in their hands they shall bear thee up, lest at any time thou dash thy foot against a stone. People Satan is full of tricks, therefore when memorizing the Word of God be careful of your correct quoting. Jesus replied, quoting the scripture, 'And Jesus answering said unto him, It is said, 'Thou shalt not tempt the Lord thy God.' After Satan tried three times and failed, he departed from Jesus for a season.

Satan in trying to deceived Jesus he used bread to fulfil 'The lust of the flesh' and failed because Jesus used the Word of God against Satan demonstrating to us that out spiritual refilling's are much more important than our physical needs in order to be conqueror over Satan and his deceptions. Secondly Satan tried to deceive Jesus to fulfil the 'Lust of the eye,' by showing Him the beauty of the world and all its contents, saying all this power is given unto me and to whom so ever I will, I give it. Satan has power but remember his power is limited, so people do not be deceived by his offering of his limited power We read in Matthews 28:18, "And Jesus came and spake unto them, saying, All power is give unto me in heaven and in earth." Jesus power has no limit, boundary, measurement neither beginning nor end. Isaiah 40: 26 reads, "Lift up your eyes on high, and behold who has created these things, that brings out their host by number: he calls them all by names by the greatness of his might, for that he is strong in power; not one fails." 1 Chronicles 29:11–12 reads, "Thine, O Lord, is the greatness, and the power, and the glory, and the majesty: for all that is in the heaven and in the earth is thine thine is the kingdom, O Lord, and thou art exalted as head over all. Both riches and honour come of thee, and thou reigns over all; and in thine hand it is to make great, and to give strength unto all." Also in Psalm, "They shall speak of the glory of thy kingdom, and talk of thy power" (Ps. 145:11).

Satan went a step feather saying just worship me and all shall be yours. Jesus responded demonstrated to us the power of the quoted 'Word of God,' saying 'for it is written, Thou shalt worship the Lord thy God, and him only shalt thou serve.' Worshipping God is a worship of 'Faith' and not by sight because the things Satan is offering are, temporal and vanity. Jesus is simply saying to us, in worshipping God, we must be whole-hearted and true in love activating our heart, soul and might, because we cannot serve two masters at the same time only one. James 4:4 reads, "Ye adulterers and adulteresses, know ye not that the friendship of the world is enmity with God? whosoever therefore will be a friend of the world is the enemy of God."

Matthew 6:19–24 says, "Lay not up for yourselves treasures upon earth, where moth and rust doth corrupt, and where thieves break through and steal."

[20] But lay up for yourselves treasures in heaven, where neither moth nor rust doth corrupt, and where thieves do not break through nor steal:

[21] For where your treasure is, there will your heart be also.

[22] The light of the body is the eye: if therefore thine eye be single, thy whole body shall be full of light.

[23] But if thine eye be evil, thy whole body shall be full of darkness. If therefore the light that is in thee be darkness, how great is that darkness!

[24] No man can serve two masters: for either he will hate the one, and love the other; or else he will hold to the one, and despise the other. Ye cannot serve God and mammon.'

We are constantly surrounded by the offering of Satan's temptations and deception on a daily basis . . . are we going to hold fast to our Faith in God, by loving and worshipping Him only? The people in Joshua's time said in Joshua 24:24, "And the people said unto Joshua, The LORD our God will we serve, and his voice will we obey."

Finally, Satan took Jesus to the top of the temple trying to deceived Him testing Him with the 'The lust of the Pride of life,' saying if you are really and truly the Son of God, cast yourself down from this height, remember angels will be present to catch you and protect you from falling. Jesus showed us we need to study the 'Word of God,' meditate on it, memorize it properly, stores it in our hearts and let God the Holy Spirit directs us how and when to use it against the deception of Satan. Remember to avoid having neither conversation nor dialog with him but just quote the Word of God as it is written and the deceiver will flee instantly. Jesus simply said, 'Thou shalt not tempt the Lord thy God. As children of God, we are going to be constantly tempted by Satan but we need to be strong in the Lord and be of good courage to overcome the deceptions and temptations of Satan. Then Satan will leave only for a season monitoring life situations looking for an open door to return with his work of deception.

Luke 4 King James Version

4 And Jesus being full of the Holy Ghost returned from Jordan, and was led by the Spirit into the wilderness,

[2] Being forty days tempted of the devil. And in those days he did eat nothing: and when they were ended, he afterward hungered.

[3] And the devil said unto him, If thou be the Son of God, command this stone that it be made bread.

[4] And Jesus answered him, saying, It is written, That man shall not live by bread alone, but by every word of God.

[5] And the devil, taking him up into an high mountain, shewed unto him all the kingdoms of the world in a moment of time.

[6] And the devil said unto him, All this power will I give thee, and the glory of them: for that is delivered unto me; and to whomsoever I will I give it.

[7] If thou therefore wilt worship me, all shall be thine.

[8] And Jesus answered and said unto him, Get thee behind me, Satan: for it is written, Thou shalt worship the Lord thy God, and him only shalt thou serve.

[9] And he brought him to Jerusalem, and set him on a pinnacle of the temple, and said unto him, If thou be the Son of God, cast thyself down from hence:

[10] For it is written, He shall give his angels charge over thee, to keep thee:

[11] And in their hands they shall bear thee up, lest at any time thou dash thy foot against a stone.

[12] And Jesus answering said unto him, It is said, Thou shalt not tempt the Lord thy God.

[13] And when the devil had ended all the temptation, he departed from him for a season.

[14] And Jesus returned in the power of the Spirit into Galilee: and there went out a fame of him through all the region round about.

[15] And he taught in their synagogues, being glorified of all.

Examples of 'Deception' of Satan among mankind.

Individual deception.

1. Satan used his old-times trick of deception destroying homes and families . . . this young man is said to be depressed and suicidal needed money, killed his mother, fled to another country, killed someone else, placed is jail, then finally deported back to his country, final results he is not fit to stand trial because he is mentally sick. Satan trick of deception, a reminder of Cain who killed his brother Abel in the beginning.

2. A group of young tourists visiting another country, Satan again causing a stirrer using deception, encouraged those (male and female) to strip themselves naked on this country's secrete mountain. Hours later an earthquake struck that mountain killing 18 people. Some of these young people were tried in the court of law, sentence and charged, then finally deported to their countries. Satan again, used deception, caused shame, disgrace and lifetime of regrets.

3. Hours later Satan used his trickery of deception destroying three well knitted closely loving families. These wives took their children on a trip, deceiving their husbands, leaving them in tears, big men hearts broken, appearing on the world-wide air waves, appealing to their wives to come home bringing their children because 'their love for them and the children remains the same.' Satan again using his tricks of deception destroying loving families.

4. Satan again using his old-time trickery of deception on man-
    kind. In the beginning he destroyed the union of 'Sweet
    Fellowship' between God the Father, God the Son, God the
    Holy Spirit with our fore-parents Adam and Eve in the Garden
    of Eden and his trend never stopped but ever continues until
    today. In the USA, Satan crept into the heart of this 21 years
    old man, who was given a gun for his 21st Birthday, using
    deception and totally destroyed his entire life, nine different
    families and endless more which we will never able to under-
    score or bring to light of our knowledge. Satan allowed him
    to pretend to be interested in their fellowship of 'Bible Study'
    as a deception to kill as many as possible which he did. Then
    boldly giving his reasons for his devilish action, the families
    of the dead ones assured him of their forgiveness to him, in
    spite of the griefs and pains they suffers because of his action
    . . . He finally showed no remorse whatsoever! People we are
    living in the last days and Satan is happily deceiving as many
    as he can to share in his judgment of torment.

5. A young man in his mid-twenties, beheaded a lady in her
    early eighties, in her own back yard with a machete, after
    just decapitating two cats during a three quarters of an hour
    rampage. This case went to court and after hearing his case,
    he was found 'Not Guilty by reason of insanity,' according to
    the reports of two psychiatrists . . . he developed an interest
    in 'shape shifters,' supernatural entities that can transform
    things and people into something else or another being. Some
    people called this behaviour locally 'seeing-spooks,' a junk
    highly intoxicated caught up in another world of imagination
    of his own. Seeing and believing things which are not so. So
    this young man it was said, saw this lady as a world known
    wicked leader (Bad Shepherd), comes back from the dead, as
    a demon in disguised. Further evidence indicated he was suf-
    fering from paranoid schizophrenia and was delusional when
    the act took place. This young man, pleaded 'Not Guilty,'
    and was said to be detained indefinitely in a special hospital
    unit. People this act was again the trickery of Satan, in the

form of deception. Satan laughs when the whole episode is completed.

6 . A man who is a millionaire went on a gambling spree, imagine, and blew approximately two to three millions on a gambling casino. This man realized he were trapped been deceived by Satan, like mother Eve in the beginning in the Garden of Eden, looked for an excuse refusing to pay up. He blamed those who invited him to the casino knowing his serious gambling admitted problem. Finally admitted he is a hopeless-addict, saying, Satan deceived him and made him do it! This man knew his weaknesses, his friends too knew his addicted problem and Satan too knew he was an easy prey to the temptation of gambling tricked him, cunningly deceived him then finally, laughed at him.

7. A student were deceived by the trickery of Satan, almost killed his teacher with a knife while he was attending to the class lesson . . . this young man finally admitted to his wrong doing. Satan laughed at this young man, who reminds us of Cain who slew his brother Abel because he acted on the deception of Satan.

8. Many politicians today refused to wait and rely on God, saying, He is not moving fast enough in accordance to their plans. Therefore, they turned their attentions to Satan asking him for his support and help. Satan gladly responded, deceiving them with his trickery, the applications of evil plans and rituals of witchcraft, magic, necromancy, sorcery, spells and obeah, gave them election victories. These results confused everyone even their own supporters and followers, asking themselves endless questions with little or no answers. The answer is evil plans + rituals = Satan victory (Curse), resulting in trouble of all sort including country and genera- tions unrest, especially among young people. People only the releasing of the power of prayer from God Almighty can dis- mantle and reverse these spells and curses of Satan, bringing peace, the restoration of joy, love, and genuine happiness to all these countries and nations. Many politicians today are

selling their souls to Satan, seeking power and authority and being destroyed by the tricks of Satan deceptions.

A quiet, cool, university student were deceived by the trickery of Satan, went on a shooting spree killing endless holiday-spree, destroying future bright hopes and plans of endless lives, families and future generations.

A woman believed her husband were unfaithful to his vow to her, allows Satan to deceived her, took her own life and all their innocent children life's as well. Satan finally laughs at her foolishness.

Many family men leaved their wives and children in search for work, from different countries migrated to the United Kingdom, were tricked and deceived by Satan to start a new family unknown to their former lawful law-abiding families in their home countries . . . destroyed many hopes, trust and dreams of untold families.

Many spiritual leaders (Bad Shepherds) allowed Satan to deceive them, who went on to deceived their faithful congregation convincing them to partake of poison drink killing everyone of all aged involved, they died and are in hell waiting their final judgment verdict, the wrath of God. People beware of the false shepherds and wolves because when that final fatal line is crossed, there is no turning back, therefore be wise . . . choose Jesus Christ and live forever!

Satan has used his best trick of deception deceiving mankind of all walks of life, saying unto them, "Whenever you become a member of my societies, your vows are none reversible, you are bound to me forever and your life is all mine!" People, let not you hearts be troubled, he is a liar, remember he is the father of lies. Have no fear his power is limited but all 'POWER' belongs to God! Therefore, you can, divorce your marriage to him, you can change your membership by saying this 'Prayer,' from your hearts to God through Jesus Christ His Son and instantly by His Power, He will 'Save you' from the pit of hell, 'Delivers you' from the hand of Satan and 'Set you free' from the awful wrath of eternal punishment with Satan. Remember to be serious and say it from your hearts. 'God's Power can make you what you ought to be, His Blood can cleanse your heart and make you free, His Love can fill your soul and you will see, 'Twas Best for Him to have His way with thee.'

I can remember during my youthful day attended Sunday school, we were taught many choruses which we sung joyously to the top of our voices, not realizing the real application and great effects of these choruses on our lives. This chorus tells us the character of Satan his aims, desires and deceptions destroying the life of men.

Satan is a sly old fox, if I catch him I'll put him in a box; lock up the box and throw away the key, for all the tricks he played on me.

WARNING! WARNING! THE PRAYER OF REPENTANCE AND ACCEPTANCE.

Jesus is coming back to this earth again, just as He promised, no one knows when, but it can be anytime. This message of climate change is God's final warning to mankind. This is the same final message God gave to Noah to the people before that final destruction.

If you do not know the Lord Jesus as your Saviour and you want to be prepared before He comes, simply say the prayer of repentance from your heart and be accepted into His Kingdom. Jesus said, we need to confess with our mouths and He will answer our prayers by forgiving us and receiving us into His Kingdom, where we will live eternally with Him.

The dying thief on the cross prayed a simple prayer, he said, "Lord remember me when thou comest into thy kingdom," then Jesus said unto him, "Verily I say unto thee. Today shalt thou be with me in paradise." You too can enter paradise by saying this prayer:

"Father, I come to you in Jesus precious name. Lord Jesus, I thank you for your presence, I know that I am a sinner and I believe that you died on the cross, shedding your precious blood for every sin which I have committed. I now open my heart and I ask you to come in and cleanse me from all my sins with your blood. Wash me, pardon me and accept me as I repent and live inside of me as I now choose to follow you. Thank you for saving me, be my Saviour, Lord and Friend in Jesus precious name Amen."

Take this prayer to everyone you know. Do not go to heaven alone, take someone with you!

St. Kitts, Nevis, and Anguilla
The Unity of the Trinity

St. Kitts is shape like a Guitar,
Nevis is shape like a Banjo,
Anguilla is shape like a Keyboard,
And this is the true identity of the Trinity musical family,
Consisting of Kittitians-Nevisians and Anguillians.

I am an Anguillian by Roots,
Without the Root there is no presence of Birth!
I am a Kittitian by Birth,
Without Birth there is no presence of Nature!
I am a Nevisian by Nature,
Without the presence of Nature, there is no evidence of Fruit,
And without the Fruit, there is no Germination and continued Generations!

The Trinity is forever harmoniously united,
Remember Unity is oneness, Unity is strength, and Unity is Power!
Unity is Love, and if God is Love, then Love is God and Unity is God.
The Trinity is harmoniously united by; sky, air, land and seas.
The Trinity is harmoniously united by; love-bonded-families, blood and nature,
The Trinity is harmoniously united by; the thrilling melody of singing,
The rhythm of sweet, skilful musical instrumental playing,
And second to none multi-national dancing.
The Trinity-Family is easily identified world-over by natural-born instinct
And character of outstanding singing, dancing and instrumental playing.

The Trinity is harmoniously united by the Dynamic Power of the Blood,
The Blood which will never ever lose its Power, it prevails forever.

The Precious Blood of Kittitians-Nevisians and Anguillians!
The Trinity family that is forever harmoniously united!

St. Kitts is famously known to the world as 'Sweet Sugar City and The Land of Beauty of the Caribbean.'
Nevis is also famously known to the world as 'Queen of the Caribbean and The Cradle of the Caribbean.'
Anguilla also is famously known to the world as 'Sea, Sun and white diamond
Sandy Beaches of the Caribbean.'
Kittitians-Nevisians and Anguillians, are all forever Blessed and Loved by the
Trinity of 'God The Father, God The Son, God The Holy Spirit'!
The Unity of The Trinity!
Author: John A Hodge.

INVITATION TO THE ENTIRE WORLD.

Come to the beautiful twin islands of St. Kitts and Nevis for your vacation, with no regrets and without delay.

My name is John Adolphus Hodge and I was born on the beautiful Island of St. Christopher. My little island inherited its name from the great voyager, Christopher Columbus, because it was the first Island he discovered in the West Indies. He was fascinated by its beauty that he left a part of his legacy by naming the Island St. Christopher. The name was later shortened to St. Kitts, as it is now commonly known. St. Kitts forms a federation with its sister island, Nevis, and both are situated in Leeward, West Indies.

The beauty of these two islands can be seen in their mountainous terrains. God has blessed us with these high mountains to signify His omnipresence and protection from the storms of nature throughout the years. The highest peak on the Island of St. Kitts is Mount Liamuiga. Liamuiga is the island's original name for its Carib inhabitants. This dormant volcano later became a safe haven for the indigenous people whose lives were threatened by the English and French settlers who both fought for total dominance of the island. It stands today as an adventurous hiking trail and an indelible reminder of the Almighty's magnificent work of creation.

While Mount Liamuiga stands prominently in St. Kitts, Nevis Peak is positioned with equal brilliance in Nevis. Centered in the middle of the Island, Nevis Peak can be seen with a white cloud settling on the peak of the mountain. It is said that this cloud looks like a Queen wearing her glittering Crown. Hence the Island's alias "Queen City." This imagery reinforces the constant presence and protection of God. Therefore, there is no argument to refute God's Divine Revelations that both St. Christopher and Nevis are forever blessed with. We are blessed! Lord, we thank you for your continuous blessings on us.

Today, if you are looking for a holiday or the most memorable vacation, look no further. I know a place where you will find both. Here are some of the numerous blessings you will experience:

- Warm weather all year round
- Sweet smiling faces
- Historical sites
- Fine hotels and guest-houses
- Exquisite cuisine
- Snorkelling and sea diving
- Rhythms of sweet steel-pan musical playing
- Forest horseback-riding
- Cultural dancing
- Boat-riding
- Mountain-hiking

Most important of all, there are churches of many faiths, where your belief can be renewed daily and true spiritual growth can manifest. The churches provide you with teachings that are rich in content and will open your heart to receive Jesus as your Saviour.

Therefore, all are welcome and cordially invited. Come one, come all, come great and small, and receive the blessings of a miracle from God. Come and be blessed with the miracle of God's creation of the Federation of St. Christopher and Nevis.

For further information, please contact the Tourist Information board at.
St Kitts: (869)-465–4040.
Fax: (869)-465-8794.
Nevis: (869)-469-7550/869-469-1042.
Fax: (869)-469-7551.

CPSIA information can be obtained
at www.ICGtesting.com
Printed in the USA
FFOW02n1753120417
34464FF